TALES AND
TRADITIONS

STORYTELLING IN
TWENTIETH-CENTURY
AMERICAN CRAFT

LLOYD E. HERMAN AND MATTHEW KANGAS

INTRODUCTION BY JOHN PERREAULT

CRAFT ALLIANCE, SAINT LOUIS
DISTRIBUTED BY UNIVERSITY OF WASHINGTON PRESS
SEATTLE AND LONDON

Tales and Traditions: Storytelling in Twentieth-Century American Craft was originated by Craft Alliance, Saint Louis, and organized in conjunction with Washington University Gallery of Art.

Distributed by University of Washington Press, Seattle and London.

"Tales and Traditions: 1750–1950" copyright © 1993 by Matthew Kangas
"Tales and Traditions: 1950–1992" copyright © 1993 by Lloyd E. Herman

Produced by Marquand Books, Inc., Seattle
Project editor: Suzanne Kotz
Managing editor: Patricia Draher
Designer: Scott Hudson
Printed and bound in St. Louis by John Stark Printing Company, Inc.

Cover: Katherine Westphal, *New Treasures of Tutankhamen* (detail), cat. no. 48
Page 2: René Clarke, *Stadium* (detail), cat. no. 12; page 8: Lillian Holm, *First Sight of New York* (detail), cat. no. 16; page 12: *Quilt* (detail), Daughters of the Grand Army of the Republic, Post 28, maker, cat. no. 6; page 32: Arturo Alonzo Sandoval, *State of the Union No. 10—Lady Liberty's Centennial Celebration* (detail), cat. no. 65.

Photo credits: Armen Photographers, cat. no. 28; Steven Cahill, cat. no. 44; Eduardo Calderón, cat. no. 68; John Carlano, cat. no. 73; Cathy Carver, cat. no. 2; Sheldan Comfert Collins, cat. nos. 31, 38; M. Lee Fatherree, cat. no. 5; Courtney Frisse, cat. nos. 23, 27; courtesy Graham Gallery, New York, cat. no. 18; Mark Greenberg, cat. no. 36; Bob Hansson, cat. no. 52; R. H. Hensleigh, cat. no. 64; Eva Heyd, cat. no. 34; Guy Mancuso, cat. no. 59; Peter Marcus, cat. nos. 70, 71; Jerry Mathiason, cat. no. 32; Steve Nelson, cat. no. 56; Ken Pelka, cat. nos. 4, 10; Jack Ramsdale, cat. nos. 1, 14, 17, 19, 24, 41; Mary S. Rezny, cat. no. 65; Schenck and Schenck, cat. no. 37; Jayme Schlepp, cat. no. 29; Larry Stein, cat. no. 54; Lewis Stewart, cat. no. 40; Sarah Wells, cat. nos. 12, 13.

CONTENTS

FOREWORD

Tales and Traditions: Storytelling in Twentieth-Century American Craft is the contribution of Craft Alliance to the celebration of 1993 as the Year of American Craft. The exhibition encompasses American craft traditions from the turn of the century to the 1990s, and we appreciate the enthusiastic support we have received from Year of American Craft organizers nationwide.

Guest curators Lloyd E. Herman and Matthew Kangas have ably produced an exhibition that fills a void that has too long existed in the field. It is our hope that this project will have a long-reaching impact on the research standards applied to the craft arts. Because the objects created by craft makers are frequently highly wrought and thus expensive, their immediate audience might seem narrow or elite. As the century draws to a close, however, many of the finest of these artworks are now in public and private collections available to the public. This exhibition draws on these newly available resources and on recent scholarship and criticism addressing the objects, and seeks to place them in a setting —the museum—where they may be visually examined, enjoyed, and seen together.

Because of obvious space limitations, we decided that the seventy-three objects included in the tour would encompass mainstream contemporary narratives in wood, fiber, metal, clay, and glass. Given these restrictions, we could not do justice to Native American and other traditional folk or ethnic craft, and the curators have recommended that they be addressed in subsequent, more specialized exhibitions.

In its many stories of personal, political, and commemorative expressions, *Tales and Traditions* is not unlike the personal history of Craft Alliance, which has grown from an affiliation of regional artists to a community-based organization serving artists, students, art collectors, and the general public. We are proud that many artists and artisans have had their first exposure through Craft Alliance, and we are pleased to celebrate the ongoing traditions of the multifaceted and ever-expanding craft movement.

We extend our gratitude to Lloyd E. Herman and Matthew Kangas, John Perreault, Joe Ketner and the Washington University Gallery of Art staff, David Smith of Smith Kramer Fine Art Services, and the many lenders who have most graciously worked with us on this exhibition. We sincerely thank the Missouri Arts Council, the Saint Louis Regional Arts Commission, the Arts and Education Council of Greater Saint Louis, and the National Endowment for the Arts for their generous support of this project, as well as the many other corporate, foundation, and individual donors (listed elsewhere in this book) who have made this exhibition possible.

James R. Reed
Executive Director

Barbara Jedda
Curator

P R E F A C E

Many museums, galleries, and private collectors contributed to the exhibition by lending either works or photographs. The institutions that graciously lent works are the American Craft Museum, New York; Chicago Historical Society; Contemporary Crafts Association, Portland, Oregon; Cooper-Hewitt National Museum of Design, Smithsonian Institution, New York; Corning Museum of Glass, New York; Craft Alliance, Saint Louis; Cranbrook Academy of Art Museum and Cranbrook Educational Community, Bloomfield Hills, Michigan; Everson Museum of Art of Syracuse and Onondaga County, New York; Flint Institute of Arts, Michigan; Los Angeles County Museum of Art; Memorial Art Gallery, University of Rochester, New York; Metropolitan Museum of Art, New York; Minnesota Museum of Art, Saint Paul; Museum of Art, Rhode Island School of Design, Providence; Museum of Modern Art, New York; National Museum of American Art, Smithsonian Institution, Washington, D.C.; National Museum of American History, Smithsonian Institution, Washington, D.C.; Nelson-Atkins Museum of Art, Kansas City, Missouri; Newark Museum, New Jersey; Oakland Museum, California; Palm Beach Community College, Florida; Scripps College, Claremont, California; and the Wood Turning Center, Philadelphia.

The private collectors and dealers who generously lent their works to the exhibition are Gretchen Adkins; Clayton Bailey; Martha Banyas; Ricky Bernstein; Dana Boussard; Dorothy May Campbell; Garth Clark and Mark Del Vecchio; William Crook; Susan Cummins Gallery, Mill Valley, California; Ray and Judy Dewey; Daphne Farago; Forbes Magazine Collection, New York; Frumkin/Adams Gallery, New York; David Furman; Charles Gailis; Martha Glowacki; Robert C. Graham, Sr.; Dellas Henke; Robert and Roberta Herman, Mrs. Virginia Holshuh; Judy Jensen; Julie: Artisans' Gallery, New York; Thomas L. and Geraldine Kerrigan; Gerhardt Knodel; the estate of Howard Kottler; Terrie Hancock Mangat; Mr. and Mrs. Randolph A. Marks; Darle and Patrick Maveety; Miller Gallery, New York; Robert Pfannebecker; Arturo Alonzo Sandoval; Judith and Martin Schwartz; Frances Senska; Tommy Simpson; Steuben Glass Company, New York; William Traver Gallery, Seattle; Mr. and Mrs. R. J. Vaccarella; Katherine Westphal; Bruce and Jacqueline Whitelam; and Virginia Wright.

The following institutions kindly provided photographs in addition to those of works in the exhibition: Arizona State University Art Museum, Tempe; Chicago Historical Society; Corning Glass Center; Cranbrook Academy of Art Museum; Everson Museum of Art of Syracuse and Onondaga County; Maryland Historical Society, Baltimore; Metropolitan Museum of Art; Museum of Art, Rhode Island School of Design; Museum of Fine Arts, Boston; and the National Museum of American History, Smithsonian Institution.

We are grateful to all the individuals at the above institutions as well as to the private collectors and dealers. Finally, we wish to thank Barbara Jedda and James Reed of Craft Alliance, Saint Louis, for inviting us to curate this exhibition. A herculean effort for all concerned, we firmly believe it was well worth the effort.

Lloyd E. Herman
Matthew Kangas

7

INTRODUCTION

As long as there are stories to be told and people who want to see as well as hear them, then paintings, photographs, sculptures, and even pots, chairs, and tapestries—all the kinds of artwork we call craft—will be used as vehicles for narrative. No surface is safe; no three-dimensional form is sacred.

Strictly speaking, a story is told in a linear mode, for, by definition, a story is a sequence of events. Storytelling through static images would logically entail the detailing of successive scenes; the cartoon strip is a familiar example. Another way is to show various actions within one frame, as in medieval paintings where the life of a saint is told through scenes deployed in one jam-packed landscape: Saint Randolph harassed by school teachers in one corner; his confrontation with art dealers a little farther toward the hills at the center; his martyrdom at the hands of his fellow-artists, who set fire to his slide sheets; and finally his ascent to heaven where he looks down upon craft makers everywhere and receives petitions for financial reward.

The viewer must know beforehand either the story or the general form of the type of story in order to reconstruct the correct narrative sequence. Obviously Saint Randolph's ascent to heaven could not come before his martyrdom. Furthermore, if the "reader" of these images had no previous experience with stories of sainthood, he or she would be totally in the dark. Clearly construction and reception or reconstruction of narrative depend upon cultural conventions. Viewers need to know how to read visual codes.

Most viewers will grasp the medieval convention of successive tableaux depicting the same character or characters at different stages of a story within one frame, but the idea that one can tell a story through an object or through a single static image is fraught with difficulties. Logic tells us that it is impossible, and yet it seems to happen all the time.

Perhaps we need to talk about the perception of narration rather than narration itself. Illusion is at the heart of all narrative, even in those stories communicated through time. Stories perpetuate the illusion that X is really the outcome of Y simply because X follows Y in time. If illusion is the basis of storytelling, then it seems less unlikely that a static image could also tell a story. But how? By suggestion, symbol, arrested action, deduction. Nevertheless, a mystery remains. Why is one picture able to convey a story, whereas another is just a picture?

If we see a picture of a cherry tree felled by an axe, we are apt to recall the fable of George Washington as a young boy. If we see a picture of a pear tree felled by an axe, we see a pear tree felled by an axe. What is the difference? If the picture of the pear tree inspired the viewer to make up a story about a pear tree felled by an axe, does the original image then qualify as a narrative image? "I lied; my sister chopped down the pear tree." "The tree was sacrificed to the goddess of pears." "The tree was felled to make way for a supermarket." Do some images inspire narrative more than others?

In his essay, Matthew Kangas touches on some ways that single, static images may be construed as narration and correctly alerts us that the viewer must actively participate. I would even further emphasize prior knowledge, for this exhibition is not about abstract narrative but about heroes, heroines, villains, and events and how they have been commemorated or emblemized in craft objects made in the United States.

The stories in this exhibition are symbolized rather than told, for in the static visual arts there is no other way to convey a story. Therefore this exhibition is about symbolic imagery in craft. In terms of art history, the cataloguing and analysis of images is not a novel approach: iconography is standard procedure. What is novel about this exhibition and its catalogue is that standard art history procedure is finally being brought to bear upon a critically and academically neglected art form—craft. Even decorative arts scholars have been remiss.

There is cause for celebration. This is not to say, however, that inquiry is now closed; we are at a beginning. Art history itself has moved into the postformalist realms of cultural theory; craft history and criticism, aided by the insights of the neighboring discipline of material culture, will no doubt follow suit, while, one hopes, firmly keeping an eye and a hand on the art objects in question. *Tales and Traditions: Storytelling in Twentieth-Century American Craft* is only one version of American craft's story. Whether intended or not, the exhibition traces craft as a vehicle for societal imagery, thus providing invaluable material for antithesis (the story of abstract craft?) and eventual synthesis—or, which is more likely, further pluralities and contradictions. One also hopes that projects such as this will stimulate more research, discourse, and critical inquiry. Craft studies must earn their place within the larger realm of art history; the objects and the artists deserve this. This will only be accomplished when no full accounting or understanding of contemporary culture excludes craft.

Beyond the remarkable profusion and persistence of "narrative" craft so amply demonstrated by the telling objects selected for this exhibition, what interests me as a critic is the question of why these objects were made. Why do artists —in this specific case, craft makers—want to tell stories? Certainly there is a market for such artworks, and this should not be too lightly dismissed either in craft or painting and sculpture. Narrative imagery can provide moral instruction and even history lessons for the literate as well as the unlettered. Reinforcement or preaching to the already converted should not be overlooked. Commemoration or memorialization is another motivation. Some craft makers understand that their work cannot be separated from political considerations, and much the same can be said for religious imagery in craft.

That a craft maker, like any artist, would yield either to a market or to individual conviction in regard to narrative imagery is not surprising. But I would suggest at least three other motivations. Storytelling is an aid to embellishment and therefore increases the attractiveness or the desirability of the object; the story dictates form. Narration is a structure and rationale for figuration; it often reaches audiences that do not understand abstraction and is therefore populist in intent. Furthermore—and this is more difficult—craft makers may be attracted to narration precisely because it is so paradoxical. It breaks one of the key formalist rules: storytelling should be left to the poets, dramatists, and novelists. Art must be about its own making. Narrative craft is an oxymoron, a contradiction in terms—and therefore all the more worth doing. It is within the realm of contradiction that all creativity begins, certainly all poetry.

Why, however, should we suppose that craft makers are different from other artists or that artists in general are different from persons who are not artists? It has been observed that human beings, for better or worse, are storytelling animals. The fireside is for storytelling, but so is the office water-cooler. More important, we tell stories to ourselves about ourselves as individuals and as cultures. Not all stories are lies.

This exhibition itself is a story of the stories in American craft. As such, what does it convey? As the selections move through time, one notices that the imagery becomes more personal or subjective. The myth of community or public language is increasingly overtaken by the myth of personal expression. Thus we confront another paradox. If storytelling in craft as in art is primarily effected by the triggering of a story the viewer already knows, how can personal narratives be conveyed? Are personal events more universal than we suppose? Are we indeed chained to each other by something called the unconscious?

Stories, even histories, begin and end as dreams. No matter how truthful it may be to say that we need stories to structure time—and therefore life—on a deeper level, we may also say that stories are timeless. Stories keep us alive. Stories can be told in static images because stories themselves are merely the vehicles for the images we define as poetry.

John Perreault
Senior Curator
American Craft Museum, New York

TALES AND TRADITIONS 1750–1950

MATTHEW

KANGAS

"Once upon a time." That is the way a story begins. There are, however, many kinds of stories, many ways to tell them, and many different reasons for telling them. Sequence or chronological development is an important part of written storytelling, and it is crucial to point out that time is often condensed in the visual arts: all elements of a tale may be present in one image. This difference immediately distinguishes the kind of storytelling or narrative found in twentieth-century American craft. Such storytelling in its broadest sense—allusion to a person, a myth, a plot, an event, a statement—provides a heretofore unseen and unappreciated dimension of achievement within the living decorative arts—or studio craft —of twentieth-century America.

Storytelling in American craft is the result of a variety of influences and purposes: social, political, historical, commemorative, personal, and psychological. It reflects the American urge to boast, brag, amuse, and tell a story about one's region, past, family, culture, or self with humor and satire, warmth and passion, anger and mystery.

Drawing upon the five basic craft materials—ceramics, glass, metals, textiles, and wood—the case for aesthetic content, or meaning, in craft can be made by a re-examination of known craft objects that never before have been grouped together or discussed in terms of their potential storytelling properties. As we shall see, craft artists, designers, and artisans often delved into pre-existing literary models for the sources of their tales: Judeo-Christian parables, Greco-Roman mythology, Arthurian legend, Shakespeare, American folklore. In addition they created their own stories, drawn from personal experience or in response to political and social events in our turbulent century. In each case, the force of the story or myth has never led to a sacrifice of craftsmanship. In fact, without excellence of execution, the story or narrative cannot be successfully carried forth.

13

Surface decoration is one vehicle for artistic content in craft. When it involves the human figure, a potential for narrative is set in motion that remains intriguing and tantalizing long after the object is made, sold, collected, and measured or assessed by art historians. An emphasis on analyzing surface decoration, however, has led to a neglect of other areas of content in twentieth-century American craft. The expropriation of the field by decorative art historians has led to an emphasis on technical, historical, and contextual aspects of craft rather than to an interpretive dimension.

This examination presumes an active interpretive faculty, going so far as to instill content where none may have been thought to exist previously. Yet in each case, the clues to interpretation occur in the physical embodiment of the artwork: imagery, juxtaposition of materials, formal properties, selection of medium. Building on these elements, it becomes possible to open up the storytelling dimension in American craft and uncover a longer lineage of high artistic purpose than has thus far been granted.

Perhaps deliberately, perhaps unwittingly, the furniture maker, the potter or clay sculptor, the glassblower or designer, the jeweler or metalsmith, and the weaver or fiber artist often present us with a potential story that weds use to meaning and, in so doing, presents his or her art in a different way than a painter or sculptor might. The story can be appreciated on many levels. And, just as various periods of history have stressed art as more or less a reflection of society, twentieth-century American craft reflects society on a much more pragmatic level.

BEFORE THE REPUBLIC

Although our focus is American craft in the twentieth century, our story begins with the origins of the Republic. One could go back even farther, to Greek vase painting, for example, or Egyptian tomb artifacts, for the roots of storytelling in craft, but, for our purposes, it is helpful to examine two contrasting works created roughly two hundred years apart.

Louis XV (fig. 1), a porcelain bust made in France at the Chantilly factory in 1745, tells no story at all; it is the embodiment of absolute power, the king of France who reigned from 1715 to 1774. The seeds of the American Revolution had been sown by French writers like Voltaire and Rousseau, but art was still consecrated to those in power. At twelve-and-one-half inches high, *Louis XV* is a diminutive symbol, made for the courtiers at Versailles or for landed aristocracy. The lion at the pedestal's base is the king of beasts, reinforcing the monarch's primary position among humans, but its tiny size renders such puissance a bit absurd.

In contrast, *Farmer and Factory Worker* (1939, fig. 2), a five-foot-high carved
stoneware sculpture by Waylande de Santis Gregory, summons up a number of
possible narratives. Heroic in its own way, it also contains symbols of power: the
earth below, a factory and smokestack, a plume of smoke. Made after the height
of the Great Depression, it poses the worker with right leg forward, ready to go.
Not a symbol of state like *Louis XV,* the sculpture is a chronicle of American corporate industrial power. On the reverse, Gregory positioned a farm worker, and
together, the two sides form a story about the range of American labor, from farm
to factory. From the ample appurtenances associated with the figures, we construct
tales about their grit, determination, sacrifice, and triumph. In a historical context,
however, a different effigy of absolute power was rising at this time: fascism.

Many stories we love are about humans and animals: Little Red Riding Hood,
Daniel in the Lion's Den, Beauty and the Beast, and others. In ancient times,
people believed gods could pose as animals to intervene with (or love or harm)
humans. The rape of Europa, a Greek myth about Zeus becoming a bull to spirit
off the lovely maiden Europa, is a mixture of violence and pastoral grace.[1] Around
1760 the Meissen workshop in Germany (where the European discovery of porcelain occurred in 1708–1709) made its own completely neutered and docile version
(fig. 3). Not threatening but delightful, it suggests how stories repeated frequently
can change radically in interpretation or reflect the context of the period in which
they are told. With European world power at an apogee, the toning down or pas-
toralization of the rape of Europa well suited an indulgent, decadent society eager
for pleasure and sensuous distractions. Garlanded with flowers, the bull—or Zeus
—and his sexual power are diminished, and satirized.

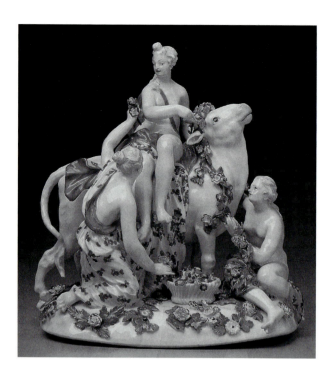 

Fig. 3. *Rape of Europa*, ca. 1760, Meissen factory, hard-paste porcelain, h. 8¹¹⁄₁₆ in., Museum of Fine Arts, Boston, bequest of Forsyth Wickes, Forsyth Wickes Collection, 65.2094.

Fig. 4. *Pitcher*, English, ca. 1810–15, earthenware, h. 6⅝ in., Metropolitan Museum of Art, gift of Eleanor G. Sargent, 1980.499.2.

Again, to demonstrate how different the American experience became, Viktor Schreckengost in *Apocalypse '42* (1942, cat. no. 25) also used an animal—a horse perched atop the world—but to a totally different end: propaganda. With Europe in flames in 1942, the Cleveland artist depicted three bloody tyrants—Benito Mussolini, Emperor Hirohito, and Adolf Hitler—seated on a horse galloping toward the end of the world, the apocalypse. Each figure is associated, like Louis XV was, with signs of his power. The helmeted skeleton among them is Death. Thus we see how similar and yet how different certain building blocks of stories can become across time.

Within the singular art object, an entire story may be told with elaborate or economical means. Sometimes the story is already familiar to the viewer. Sometimes the viewer must create the story out of the elements provided. In emblematic objects, one image might stand for the whole story. In functional objects, the object's use might complete the story told on its surface. Where many images are present, more than one story might be told simultaneously, like reading a short story anthology all at once.

Any traditional story requires a teller, and, in our case, the teller is the art object. It is the carrier or mediator of the story between the artist and the viewer. In the same way that the bull and the horse are carriers of their characters, so any crafted artwork is the vehicle for the story its maker chooses to convey.

The person hearing a tale or the audience looking at an object also participates in how the story is imparted. We bring our own wealth of experiences as individuals to each story we see or hear; we also participate collectively as an audience, as in the theater, responding as a group to certain commemorative portraits, for example, of our national leaders. Depending on the audience and the particular point in time, then, the story's impact and meaning may change. *Apocalypse '42* had an entirely different meaning—a warning—when it was first made in 1942. By then the United States had a fully established national identity, and

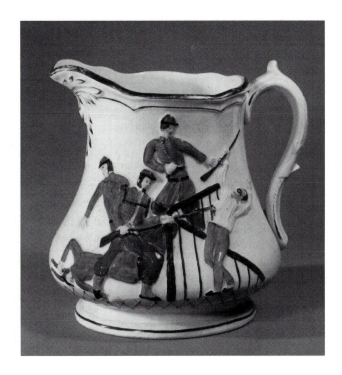

Fig. 5. *Covered jug,* Chinese export ware, Qing dynasty, ca. 1805, glazed pottery, h. 10 in., Metropolitan Museum of Art, Harris Brisbane Dick Fund, 34.74a,b.

Fig. 6. *Pitcher,* ca. 1861, Millington, Astbury, and Paulson, maker, porcelain, h. 8 in., Metropolitan Museum of Art, gift of Florence I. Balasny-Barnes, in memory of her sister, Yvette B. Gould, 1984.443.1.

the artist responded to the threat posed by military aggression abroad to that way of life and its values.

Long before, when the Republic was young, much of the lore that established the American identity was promulgated in craft objects manufactured in England (fig. 4), France, Germany, and China (fig. 5) and exported to the ex–North American colonies. Often the subject matter dealt with American themes, military heroes, and victors. In a pitcher made in America (fig. 6), even a traitor was memorialized. Basic utilitarian wares of clay, wood, metal, glass, and cloth were produced in the young nation, but fine decorative objects were not made extensively. To be sure, magnificent examples of silver from New York or Boston were extant as early as the seventeenth century; the silversmiths were usually of Dutch (New York) or French origin (for example, Paul Revere, the Boston silversmith and subject of his own Americana myth).

When foreign trade was renewed after the Revolutionary War, Americans set about furnishing their homes by, for example, ordering dinnerware from as far away as Nanjing, China. The household wares imported from abroad by George Washington, for instance, have been the subject of extensive research.[2] It was English and French artisans, however, who shepherded ahead American craft makers by the examples of their superlative workmanship and highly developed way of telling a story—and decorating a useful object at the same time.

BEFORE THE "AMERICAN CENTURY"

When I peruse the conquer'd fame of heroes
and the victories of mighty generals,
I do not envy the generals,
Nor the President in his Presidency, nor the
rich in his great house . . .

—WALT WHITMAN, *from "When I Peruse the Conquer'd*
Fame" (1860)

It was the founder of Time, Inc., Henry B. Luce, who coined the term "American century" in a February 1941 issue of *Life* magazine.[3] Regardless of its appeal and widespread adherence, the concept of the American century also carried implications of military and moral domination. Many of the objects considered in this catalogue conform to or refute that vision of America as rightly all-powerful. Before examining them, it is worthwhile to scan briefly some high points of nineteenth-century American craft. Although midcentury American power brokers like Luce claimed the twentieth century as the apogee of U.S. power, events of the nineteenth century also accumulated into an overwhelming sense of confidence, pride, and even arrogance.

The Civil War, to be sure, wrenched the nation, but it also led to extraordinary industrial growth in the North after the war. Add to that the westward expansion both before and after the Civil War, the fulfillment of Manifest Destiny (another shibboleth of inevitable American power), and the conquering of Native American peoples. The perception of a God-given right to prosperity despite human and ecological costs became palpable.

The spoils of the Industrial Revolution were garnered primarily in the East. Like Napoleon crowning himself emperor, American industrial leaders, through related cultural agents and institutions, commemorated their achievements, such as the expansion of the railroad, with objects of commanding beauty and richness (fig. 7).

The centennial year of 1876 was a stock-taking time for the nation. At the Centennial Exposition in Philadelphia, the accomplishments of national craft artists were put on view, and many pottery companies, for example, prepared exhibits or created works especially for the occasion. Chief among these was the *Century Vase* (1877, fig. 8)[4] designed by Karl L. H. Müller for his employer, Union Porcelain Works, at Greenpoint in Brooklyn, New York.

While President Washington presides over the vase from a portrait medallion, a narrative of American power, done in the style of Greek vase scenes, unfolds along the base. Scenes of Native Americans, a Revolutionary War soldier, and the Boston Tea Party are among those abbreviated into instantly recognizable stories, which, when taken together, form a grand narrative of the Republic up to that time.

Significant for its execution in porcelain (placing the United States on a footing with Europe and Asia), the *Century Vase* tells a story whose meaning has changed with the passing of time. Looking back, the Indians seem glorified as another vanquished and submissive enemy, and the bison-head handles remind us of the slaughter of bison and buffalo that went hand in hand with the opening of the Far West. What was celebrated then might be mourned today. Nevertheless, the vase remains a high point for American craft.[5]

If the story of the railroads, the conquering of Native Americans, and the glories of the first century of independence were celebrated on decorative objects, it is safe to say that capitalist entrepreneurship was the underlying driving force in American craft at this time. Patronage determines content in art, and the robber barons and new American millionaires of the post–Civil War Gilded Age were well equipped to commission domestic interiors by Tiffany,[6] portraits by William Merritt Chase, and a whole panoply of magnificently useless objects, the kinds of things that Harvard economist Thorstein Veblen alluded to as "conspicuous consumption" in his 1899 study, *The Theory of the Leisure Class.*[7]

BEFORE THE GREAT WAR

The nineteenth century did not really end until 1918, with the end of World War I. At that time the confidence and complacent isolation of the American Republic were shattered, along with strict behavioral conventions and moral attitudes that had been the hallmarks of a long stretch of peace, a monopolistic system of commodity distribution, and an unparalleled growth of wealth.

American craft benefited from a renewed appreciation of the handmade in the face of the factory-made and from the generosity of industrial satraps who, having traveled in Europe, were eager to prove the equal abilities of American artisans. From 1890 to 1914, the last period of innocent national confidence before the wholesale slaughter abroad, a free-spending atmosphere generated commissions for elaborately fashioned decorative objects which often had stories of their own to reveal.

Made over a two-year period, the so-called *Adams Vase* (1893–95, fig. 9), was sold by Tiffany and Company but designed by Paulding Farnham. Presented to Edward Dean Adams, chairman of the board of the American Cotton Oil Company, it is constructed of solid gold, sterling silver, pearls, enamel, and semi-precious stones. Once again, American craft makers catered to the aggrandizement of a patron, in this case, the giant cotton industry, whose insistence on slavery had been one cause of the Civil War.

The *Adams Vase*, made within thirty years of the South's defeat, presents an idealized vision of the product that produced a few millionaires but caused the suffering and death of thousands. The vase represents a cotton plant in form, with tendrils rising from the "earth" at its base and personifications of Greek mythological figures such as Mercury flanking either side. Two seated youths perched on the base are reminiscent of the figures of Italian Renaissance goldsmith and sculptor Benvenuto Cellini.

Cotton bolls are emulated by pearls contained in golden leaves. Four golden eagles surmount the shoulders of the vase. Immediately recognizable as symbols of America, the eagles also remind us that a gold eagle-coin was issued by the U.S. Treasury during this period. As such, America-as-eagle is indistinguishable from wealth or money.

In fact, every aspect of the vase and each of its story elements conspire to present an idealized image of labor. In ironic contrast to King Cotton's origins as slaveholder, the figures exist in a deified, carefree state. With the gold marvelously entangling the vessel and literally overgrowing it, a tale of ensnarled plantations, divided loyalties, and ruthlessly encroaching brokers (like Adams?) operates on a darker, subterranean level. The *Adams Vase* is an orgy of capitalistic self-congratulation typical of the era before the Great War.

If African-Americans were removed from the story of cotton in the *Adams Vase*, they were sure to be represented—and frequently condescended to—in the coming century. Long before happy-go-lucky stories about blacks appeared in American craft, Native American peoples were subjected to hypocritically romantic treatment of their own. Free-spirited but vanquished, and therefore targets for sentimentalized mythology, various indigenous tribes appeared on decorative arts objects, such as the Rookwood vase depicting Chief Joseph of the Nez Percé tribe of Idaho, Montana, and Washington (fig. 10), painted by William P. McDonald (see also cat. nos. 7, 14). Contained, if not doomed, by a

European form (the porcelain vase), Chief Joseph barely emerges from the darkened ground, as if he and the Nez Percé were already consigned to oblivion. Although McDonald's likeness is not based on the known photograph by Edward S. Curtis, it was Curtis who drew Easterners' attention to the great leader. He wrote to University of Washington President Edmond S. Meany at the time of Chief Joseph's death in 1904:

> At last his long, endless fight for his return to the old home is at an end . . . Perhaps he was not quite what we in our minds had pictured him but I still think that he was one of the greatest men that has ever lived.[8]

If the Indian wars were being consigned to narratives of one-sided nostalgia, Civil War wounds were still raw as late as 1908. When can a craft work look like a storytelling device but not really be one? A quilt at the Chicago Historical Society, made by Post 28 of the Daughters of the Grand Army of the Republic (1907–1908, cat. no. 6), includes all the discrete elements of storytelling—pictures, words, sequential arrangements—without a fully developed tale. Its composition situates each regimental memorial emblem close to another, approximating the logic of a story. But we re-create by inference the stories of the men killed and their diverse national and geographic origins. In this sense the quilt foretells the major memorial quilt of the late twentieth-century, the *AIDS Memorial Quilt* (see Herman, below, fig. 2), which, like the Civil War quilt, is the work of many hands. Each panel represents an individual dead from AIDS, but, taken together, there is no specific story other than their shared tragedies.

Furniture makers on the East and West Coasts actively participated in the creation of stories carved into domestic objects like hope chests and library desks (fig. 11, cat. nos. 2, 5). Influenced by the adulation of John Ruskin and William

Morris for the medieval English craftsman and his union of art and labor, American painter Sydney Richmond Burleigh designed the *King Arthur Chest* (ca. 1900, cat. no. 2) and the *Shakespeare Chest* (ca. 1900, fig. 11) for the cabinetmakers Potter and Company. Both works embody fascinating treatments of popular stories.[9]

The *King Arthur Chest,* carved by Julia Lippitt Mauran, is, appropriately, adorned by King Arthur and his queen, Guinevere. Surrounding them on the end and back panels are not the figures of the Knights of the Round Table but their names, coats-of-arms, and related attributes. On one end of the chest is the familiar helmet of Sir Lancelot; at the other end, the name of his son, Galahad, is joined by the Holy Grail, which he recaptured according to legend. The original collection of tales, Sir Thomas Malory's 1469 *Le Morte d'Arthur,* was given new currency in Tennyson's popular series of poems *Idylls of the King,* which appeared between 1859 and 1872. Readers undoubtedly appreciated Burleigh and Mauran's shorthand combination of all the characters of the stories in one work, constructing, as in a totem pole, a three-dimensional literary entity.

More complicated in that it exposes many characters from different plays, the *Shakespeare Chest* (fig. 11) tells us much about which plays were deemed most appropriate to commemorate: *Taming of the Shrew, As You Like It, Merry Wives of Windsor,* and *Antony and Cleopatra*—three comedies and a tragedy. Strong female characters dominate each play, and, indeed, Cleopatra is depicted alone, resplendent on her throne. Furniture as literary anthology is the underlying narrative principle of this chest rather than a series of individual plot elements tied together within one object.

The *Shakespeare Chest* was carved by Arthur Mathews, whose wife, Lucia Kleinhans Mathews, assisted in choosing colors and in some of the painting and carving.[10] Real collaborators, the Mathewses had their own retail outlet, The Furniture Shop, at 1717 California Street in San Francisco. Inspired by Italian Renaissance painting and furniture, Arthur and Lucia Mathews made richly painted and carved wooden objects of all sizes and types (cat. no. 5), furnishing and supplying the large new mansions of the Bay Area's burgeoning ruling class of merchants, shipping magnates, and financial leaders.

Works in glass perpetuated myths of triumph and progress that drove the nation forward in an unquestioning pursuit of land, power, wealth, and self-satisfaction (cat. nos. 3, 8). A small masterpiece of engraved glass, *Apotheosis of Transportation* (fig. 12), by Hieronimus William Fritchie, was displayed by the Libbey Glass Company at the 1904 Louisiana Purchase Exposition in Saint Louis. Exuberant, rambunctious, and absurd, it combines horses, mermaids, a demigod, and even the zodiac in a stunning composition around a world globe with a map of the United States near the plate's exact center. More than a tribute to sea travel, railroads, or horseback riding, this work foretells America's presence abroad, and, like some other narrative craft objects, it unwittingly anticipates darker adventures of American empire building in the dawning century.

In a final irony on the memory of the young Republic, now long gone, Tiffany Furnaces used the Liberty Bell suspended in the talons of an eagle as a symbol for the victory over Germany in 1918 (cat. no. 8), avoiding any allusion to the hundreds of thousands killed. This souvenir bowl made of iridescent gold glass reminds us with an eerie glow of the generous profits made during World War I by the last of the pre–income tax capitalists, the munitions manufacturers, who stayed home.

The Great War was over, and only with its conclusion did the nineteenth century come to an end. Chastened by loss but liberated from Victorian convention, President Woodrow Wilson's America was ready to escape into a frenzy of consumption. Craft artists would cooperate fully in telling the stories Americans wanted to hear, drowning out the accounts of starvation, inflation, and economic collapse coming from Europe.

PLEASURE AND PROSPERITY

We were very tired, we were very merry—
We had gone back and forth all night on the ferry.
We hailed, "Good morrow, mother!" to a shawl-covered head,
And bought a morning paper, which neither of us read;
And she wept, "God bless you!" for the apples and pears,
And we gave her all our money but our subway fares.
—EDNA ST. VINCENT MILLAY, *from*
"Recuerdo" (1922)

The interwar period, from 1919 to 1939, was an economically divided time, prosperity followed by the Great Depression, yet much American craft remained at the level of fantasy and escape. Painting and sculpture perhaps more clearly reflected coming hard times, but American craft with few exceptions (cat. no. 21) took a position of soothing detachment from the sobering conditions.

At first there was a comfortable congruity between life-style and imagery. John Held, Jr., the great illustrator of the age of F. Scott Fitzgerald, joined René Clarke and others in designing fabric patterns for Stehli Prints (cat. nos. 12, 13) which celebrated jazz and the growing mania for varsity athletics and baseball. Held's *Rhapsody* (1927, cat. no. 13) was printed in blue dye, punning the title of George Gershwin's composition for piano and orchestra, "Rhapsody in Blue" (1924). In Held's design, the musicians play violins, tubas, banjo, tympana, piano, and other instruments; the repeated orchestra pattern of circular forms resembling musical notes (cymbals, bass drums, heads, trombone bells) sets up a syncopated visual rhythm similar to jazz. The cumulative effect tells a story of the interface between jazz and classical music that occurred in the 1920s and in Gershwin's music.

Immigration increased as a result of growing storms over Europe, although isolationist figures like aviator Charles Lindbergh and diplomat Joseph P. Kennedy, Sr., were firmly opposed to any American intervention abroad. The growing presence of Asian peoples on the West Coast was symbolized in a stoneware sculpture of 1921 by Italian immigrant Beniamino B. Bufano, who had settled in San Francisco earlier in the century. In *Chinese Man and Woman* (cat. no. 9), two figures, solemnly staring forward, are dressed in traditional clothing replete with embroidered Chinese characters. Their exotic features and attire place them in a category by now common to American craft, the outsider. As dominant a part of the Bay Area's economy as they were, Asians were treated by craft as "others," fit subject matter for diminutive (thirty-one inches high) execution.

The American Indian had already been subjected to this aesthetic colonization and would continue to be treated so, as in the baptismal font decoration for Christ Church Cranbrook in Bloomfield Hills, Michigan (cat. no. 14). The Indian brave, drawn by Victor F. von Lossberg for the New York firm of Edward F. Caldwell and Company in 1927, is joined by other figures surrounding the font, including representations of Africa (a black man with bird and lion), Asia (a robed Asian with birds and blossoms), and Europe (a bearded figure with a book and grape leaves). America, then, is embodied by the Christianized Indian worshiping the European God, with upturned palms in a degradingly supplicatory pose. The characters on the font may be multicultural, but like much other art of the period, such representations rest on racial stereotyping and subordination to a dominant white culture.

If the United States received new citizens from abroad who brought their considerable skills with them (indeed, virtually the entire early faculty and administration of the Cranbrook Academy of Art, founded in 1925, are a good example of this), native-born artists in turn took advantage of superior craftsmanship available in Europe. *At the Gates of Morning* (ca. 1925, cat. no. 11) by painter Arthur B. Davies, for example, was executed at the Gobelins tapestry factory in France: no adequate American institution existed at the time to create a tapestry on this scale.

By 1932, however, Eliel and Loja Saarinen had arrived in Bloomfield Hills, Michigan, to transfer their Finnish-trained skills in architecture, weaving, and art school administration to Cranbrook.[11] In *Sample for the Festival of the May Queen Hanging* (1932, cat. no. 19), the Saarinens imported pagan festival imagery to America. Here and in other works, European cultural traditions, such as those dealing with seasonal planting cycles, were monumentalized and made to constitute a neutral, nonideological educational philosophy for the art school.

Lillian Holm epitomized the European immigration experience in her large weaving *First Sight of New York* (early 1930s, cat. no. 16). With skyscrapers looming overhead and a crush of people on either side, Holm's surrounding pattern of windowlike rectangles and inverted triangles continues the jazzy rhythm set up in *Rhapsody* (cat. no. 13). She accentuated the separateness of the outsiders looking in by placing red horizontal lines across the image; the lines seem more a barrier to the American dream than a conduit to it.

Two ceramic vignettes, *Ten Nights in a Bar Room* (1932, cat. no. 18) by Henry Varnum Poor and *Futility of a Well-ordered Life* (1935, cat. no. 21) by Russell Barnett Aitken, also comment on the dark side of the depression. The former satirizes Prohibition through a scene from the popular Victorian melodrama *Ten Nights in a Bar Room and What I Saw There* (1854), by Timothy Shay Arthur and William W. Pratt. Poor's tableau approximates a proscenium stage set with its curved front but also splits the scene in two by topping the sculpture with a glimpse of nearby tenements. It could be that the moment captured, of a drunk collapsing, alludes to the play's climactic line, "Father, dear father, come home with me now." Made during the height of the "great experiment," *Ten Nights* would have been viewed by Poor's audience with a mixture of sophistication and sarcasm rather than the moral righteousness and approval of Arthur and Pratt's original theatergoers. It is a good example of transplanted narrative, always subject to the shifting allegiances and biases of those who hear the story at a different time in history.

Fig. 14. Waylande de Santis Gregory, *Fountain of the Atom: Electron,* 1938, stoneware, h. 46 in., Cranbrook Academy of Art Museum, lent by Jerome and Patricia Shaw. Photo: Jack Ramsdale.

With the New York World's Fair in 1939–40, large-scale commissions gave American craft makers a number of opportunities to tell stories using craft materials. Despite the coming horrors abroad, brash optimism was the order of the day, and allegory—a story that exists on different levels of meaning with each character or plot standing in for something else—was a preferred storytelling vehicle.

For the Glass Industries Building, Steuben designer Sidney Waugh created *Atlantica* (1938–39, fig. 13). Executed in cast colorless glass, *Atlantica* is the result of several months' work and required the involvement of many technicians and workers. With the mermaid's hair echoing the surrounding wave forms, *Atlantica* is not that different in form from heroic, Nazi-period sculptures aggrandizing the Aryan race, which were produced in Germany by artists such as Arno Breker. Grand, imposing, and imperious, *Atlantica*, as corporate power feminized, was also a symbol for the achievements of Corning Glass Company and Steuben, a subsidiary. She may have allegorically represented the ocean connecting North America and Europe, but that body of water was soon to be dotted with German U-boats, sunken transport ships, and all manner of peril politely absent from Waugh's design.

Equally optimistic and chilling in its implications, *Fountain of the Atom: Electron* (1938, fig. 14) by Waylande de Santis Gregory, played on the fair's theme of "Building the World of Tomorrow with the Tools of Today." Electrons were allegorized into innocent children and joined by monumental figures of fire, earth, air, and water, the basic elements first conceived of by the ancient Greeks. Just a few years later, such benign storytelling would be undercut by the bombs dropped on Hiroshima and Nagasaki, not to mention the subsequent nuclear weapons build-up of the Cold War.

Analogous to *Atlantica,* another sculpture of the same era, *Earth* (1939, cat. no. 23), personified the planet as a beautiful, dark-skinned woman. Artist Edris

Eckhardt created many sculptures dealing with children's storybook figures, and her ability to conflate narrative elements or attributes into a single figure serves her well in this piece. With her blue-green hair in the form of the ocean's waves, *Earth* answers the sinuous water forms of *Atlantica* and appears equally innocent of any sinister meaning. Viewed from our own day of ecological cataclysms, *Earth,* like much art of the late 1930s, seems impossibly naive. Nevertheless, the considerable beauty and exquisite workmanship of these works redeem them up to a point and remind us that a literal reflection of society's ills is not always desired by patronage.

With the coming of World War II, the pursuit of pleasure that had begun in the 1920s and which was perpetuated in craft objects of the 1930s—despite the depression—gave way to images of power and domination. New stories of military triumph would replace tales of pastoral bliss, scientistic faith, and the subordination of outsiders.

MYTHOLOGIES OF POWER

The dove descending breaks the air
With flame of incandescent terror
Of which the tongues declare
The one discharge from sin and error . . .
— T.S. ELIOT, *from "Little Gidding," in* Four Quartets *(1942)*

T. S. Eliot's lines were written during the London Blitz and probably refer to the unrelenting bombing of the city by German planes. His cloaking of World War II's horror in quasi-religious language was just one of many responses to the war by which American artists generally avoided the explicit reality of current events.

Even if not commenting on the crimes of the Axis powers, some artists were strangely close in spirit to the heroic fascist style. *Man and the Unicorn* (1940, fig. 15) by Swedish sculptor Carl Milles, for example, parallels male domination fantasies evoked by the work of Nazi-period artists. In this case, the myth of the free, independent unicorn—whom no one could catch—is perverted into a tale of mastery over the creative spirit. It is a celebration of dominance with the ridiculously muscled rider seated on the back of the tense, subdued animal. Milles's extraordinary wood carving sets in motion troubling scenarios about psychological states as well, perhaps the triumph of the ego over the id. Natural forms, such as the vegetation at the unicorn's hooves, are threatening and entangling, too.

Perpetuating a mythology of power at a time when America was uncertain about involvement in Europe, Steuben designer Sidney Waugh matched his *Atlantica* with *The Bowl of American Legends* (1942, cat. no. 26), a medley of homegrown stories about dominance in all regions of the country. Blown and

Fig. 15. Carl Milles, *Man and the Unicorn*, 1940, carved wood, h. 49 in., Cranbrook Academy of Art Museum, gift of Carl Milles, CAAM 1944.21. Photo: Jack Ramsdale.

engraved at the Steuben furnaces in Corning, New York, the clear crystal rises in a single curve from a disklike base. Repeating the oldest of all narrative structures for craft, a band around a vessel, Waugh designed a nonsequential series of images which blend together into a continuum of "legendary and semi-legendary characters"[12] intricately tied to national fantasies about the South, New England, the Midwest, Far West, and Texas.

Rip Van Winkle, Ichabod Crane, and the Headless Horseman remind us that Washington Irving's writings were part polished prose, part fatuous lore. Joel Chandler Harris, another writer associated with condescending racial stereotypes, is represented by Uncle Remus, Br'er Rabbit, and Br'er Fox. Johnny Appleseed, presaging America's agri-business perhaps, grew out of the Ohio territories, and Paul Bunyan, according to Waugh, "brings us to the great days of the opening of the West."[13] Completing the bowl's circular band, Pecos Bill and Davy Crockett—"in fact, a member of Congress"[14]—blur the line between fantasy and reality and remind us of a cardinal aspect of American craft storytelling: escapist tales must blend with patriotic myths to ensure popularity, and consumption.

Viktor Schreckengost's *Apocalypse '42* (cat. no. 25), a scary blend of humor and reality, remains the paramount topical craft achievement of the era just before World War II. But then, Schreckengost's vision grew out of his experience as an American tourist in pre-war Germany. Along with other boat passengers arriving in Lübeck harbor from Sweden, he was briefly sequestered before being allowed to proceed southward. Peeking out a window while being held, he saw dozens of airplanes "in full war paint"[15] and knew firsthand what the near future would inexorably bring.

Fig. 16. Russell Barnett Aitken, *Mussolini, Hitler,* and *Roosevelt,* ca. 1939–40, stoneware, Arizona State University Art Museum, 82.3–5.

Five years later, when *Apocalypse '42* was first shown at the Cleveland Art Museum, Schreckengost was surprised when the work was ostensibly removed for photography. Upon inquiring further, the artist learned that members of Cleveland's large Italian-American community had objected to the sculpture's depiction of Mussolini sliding off a horse's rump. The dictator had apparently presented awards to some supporters then resident in the Cleveland area. Eventually the work was returned to the exhibition area by the museum director.

Three stoneware figures made about the same time by Russell Barnett Aitken (fig. 16) form a beautiful pendant to Schreckengost's unitary sculpture. For Aitken, each individual statuette contains explanatory attributes. *Mussolini* is the target of a nose-thumbing African, symbolizing invaded Abyssinia. *Hitler* holds a copy of *Mein Kampf* and wears a Viking cap. A blonde-braided Rhine maiden crouches at his feet. And in a twist away from Schreckengost, Aitken, in *Roosevelt,* makes a subtle dig at the president's own possible military yearnings by garbing him as an admiral, alluding to his former post as Assistant Secretary of Navy.

After the war, the nation returned to deeply conservative values embodied in the Judeo-Christian tradition. These were the values, after all, that the Allies had fought to preserve in the face of Nazi barbarism and the extermination of European Jewry.

Three works, two in clay and one in metal, demonstrate the perpetuation of storytelling in American craft up to midcentury. The earliest, *Triptych with Virgin and Child* (ca. 1940, cat. no. 24) by Arthur Nevill Kirk, is barely ten inches high, yet it attains a monumentality that bears comparison to the great medieval enamels of Limoges. With readily recognizable figures of the Magi and shepherds flanking Mother and Child, this work underscores the continuity of both high craftsmanship and high narrative content in twentieth-century American craft. A myth of power in its own way, *Triptych* still presents an image of gentle authority and modest assertion.

In contrast, *Carved Bowl (Passion of Christ)* (1947, cat. no. 27) by Thomas McClure seems more Christianized than Christian myth with its crude paganlike relief carving. Through elaborate interlocking sections, the story of Christ's betrayal, crucifixion, and return are told in a blunt, wraparound sequence. It is almost as if, after the horrors of World War II, a more refined execution would be unseemly. Unglazed, the bowl compresses its story dramatically, like French Romanesque cathedral sculpture, but, confined to a clay pot, the Passion reverts to the symbolic ritual of preliterate cultures, becoming a powerfully expressionistic portrayal of sacrifice and renewal.

Judgment of Solomon (1948, cat. no. 28) by Edwin and Mary Scheier attains a remarkable concision in its balancing of Old Testament story elements, all seen simultaneously on a plate. Executed in Durham, New Hampshire, *Judgment of Solomon* firmly illustrates the notion of the craft object as narrator. With one hand raised in a contemplative pose and his scepter in the other, King Solomon adjudicates a dispute between two women fighting over possession of an infant son. Literally depicted as embodiments of his memory, the three figures are positioned in the king's head; we are experiencing Solomon's deliberations prior to his decision.

The Scheiers were self-taught artists when they began making ceramics in 1937, and much of the freshness of the drawing on the plate rises from its self-invented style, reinforcing, again, the preliterate sensibility found in McClure's *Passion of Christ.* Viewed in the context of renewed American power after the war, the Scheier plate proposes a newfound wisdom for the United States as the country took its place in the United Nations, the new world forum of diplomacy, decision, and judgment. Although Edwin Scheier denies a conscious link to such developments at the time he made the plate, in retrospect he freely admits the possibility of such an analogy.[16]

Despite judicious efforts at serious moral subject matter by the Scheiers, McClure, and Kirk, and the explicitly engaged political satires of Poor, Schreckengost, and Aitken, by and large American craft participated in reinforcing helpful illusions about how Americans would like to see themselves as a nation. Rather than reflecting the country's problems, American craft of the first half of the twentieth century prepared the way for artists of the second half to react profoundly against such elegant escapism. The stories that would be told next were created by artists who withdrew even more or who expressed increasing doubts about America's confidence in its values and political power in the Cold War era.

We shall not cease from exploration
And the end of all our exploring
Will be to arrive where we started
And know the place for the first time.

—T.S. ELIOT, *from "Little Gidding," in* Four Quartets *(1942)*

NOTES

1. Robert Graves, *The Greek Myths: 1* (London: Penguin Books, 1955), 194–95.
2. Susan Gray Detweiler, *George Washington's Chinaware* (New York: Harry N. Abrams, 1982).
3. John B. Judis, *Grand Illusion: Critics and Champions of the American Century* (New York: Farrar, Straus and Giroux, 1992).
4. John Spargo, *Early American Pottery and China* (Garden City, N.Y.: Garden City Publishing, 1926), 284–85.
5. An even more elaborate version which includes scenes of telegraph lines being erected is in the collection of the Brooklyn Museum; see Garth Clark, *American Ceramics: 1876 to the Present,* revised ed. (London: Booth-Clibborn Editions, 1979), 12–13.
6. Frances Weitzenhoffer, *The Havemeyers: Impressionism Comes to America* (New York: Harry N. Abrams, 1986).
7. Thorstein Veblen, *The Theory of the Leisure Class* (New York: Macmillan, 1899).
8. Barbara A. Davis, *Edward S. Curtis: The Life and Times of a Shadow Catcher* (San Francisco: Chronicle Books, 1985), 39.
9. Wendy Kaplan, *The Art That Is Life: The Arts & Crafts Movement in America 1875–1920* (Boston: Museum of Fine Arts, 1987), 142–43.
10. Ibid., 191–92.
11. Joan Marter et al., *Design in America: The Cranbrook Vision 1925–1950* (Detroit: Detroit Institute of Arts, 1983), 184.
12. Sidney Waugh, "The Bowl of American Legends," interview transcript in Corning Museum Archives.
13. Ibid.
14. Ibid.
15. Conversation with author, August 28, 1992.
16. Conversation with author, September 1, 1992.

TALES AND TRADITIONS 1950–1992

LLOYD E.

HERMAN

Everybody knows a story. Small stories—childhood make-believe, family anecdotes, neighborhood gossip—and tales as grand as myths and epic histories. Stories are in each of our memories and influence how we think and live. In the United States, although we may read the *Iliad* and the *Odyssey*, or know of Finland's epic *Karavala* or India's *Mahabharata,* we have no unifying national literary epic. Instead, accepting—even treasuring—our diversity as immigrants to a new land, we are open to the experiences that form new stories.

The most familiar stories may be those about the founding of this nation more than two hundred years ago, the hardships faced by our pioneering forebears as they forged westward in search of opportunity, the quest for racial equality and civil rights within this century, or the tribulations of recent immigrants as they struggle to fit in. The Bible, the Bill of Rights, the family photo album, and the evening news are other sources of stories.

Storytelling has not always played a large role in American craft, however rich in the history of world art are tapestries and stained-glass windows. The role of craft—objects made by hand of clay, glass, wood, fiber, leather, or metal—was usually a homely one in the early years of this nation. North American colonists had to make or have made functional wares that they could not bring with them or import. Consequently men and women learned to spin flax into linen thread and wool into yarn and to weave their threads into fabric for clothing, bedclothes, and curtains. Worn-out clothes were woven or braided into rugs or pieced into wonderful quilts. Among the most visible narrative aspects of American folk craft traditions are those quilts depicting Bible stories or stitched with the signatures of the maker's friends.

33

After serving for years as necessities, handmade objects declined in importance as America industrialized. The American Arts and Crafts movement, at its zenith in the 1880s and 1890s, was terminated by World War I and the shortages of materials and declining markets for luxury goods. Although the British social reformers who founded the movement in England had hoped to restore dignity to the work of the hand, the expensive, simply designed wares were largely supported by an elite market.

The handmade aesthetic object—functional or not—was infused with new energy by European immigrants in the 1940s. Textiles surely led the way, with Jean Lurçat's revival of tapestry weaving in France in the 1930s. His wall hangings often were of stylized figures, but they did not usually—if ever—include explicit narrative or portraiture. Dorothy Liebes, the American weaver known for her unorthodox color combinations and use of metallic plastics, as early as 1936 had made *Schiaparelli,* a woven wall hanging that recalled abstractly the famous Parisian fashion designer by integrating cloth measuring tapes and metallic dressmaker's shears. Liebes's refreshing sense of portraiture was hardly a trend, however. Most craft objects made into the 1950s incorporated human figures only as decorative elements, however much we might wish them to signal stories. For example, Lenore Tawney's gossamer wall hanging, *Bound Man* (1957, cat. no. 31), evokes a prisoner of some sort, his bound hands creating tension along the lines of the body, but the artist disclaims an explicit story line.[1]

In the spirit of national optimism that marked the 1950s, crafts embraced modern times as surely as did manufacturing, home building, and fashion design. Few craft makers had been able to sustain hand production during wartime. Ceramics had declined to a "backyard" industry; furniture making would not become a major craft occupation until the 1970s; and glass was virtually unknown as a material suitable for an artist's creativity.

When the war ended, the G.I. Bill made college education available to returning veterans. New courses in craft materials and processes were often taught in the art department rather than industrial education or home economics. Important to the development of figurative craft, basic drawing and painting were among the skills that students were taught, or with which they could experiment. The rendering of the human figure and other realistic elements of pictorial art were essential to making storytelling objects. Many graduating craft makers became teachers in an expanding number of university craft programs, and some practitioners of this period soon became legendary in their media.

In the 1950s, the posed figure became a player in a scene. The Montana potter Peter Voulkos was already known in the early part of the decade for his masterfully thrown large pots and jars. When he used figures in their decoration, they were often abstracted human or animal forms. *Babe, the Blue Ox* (ca. 1952, cat. no. 30) is one of very few examples that rely on folklore as the subject of such decoration. The famous ox owned by the legendary woodsman Paul Bunyan is a recurring figure in the tales of the great north woods of Michigan and Wisconsin and was borrowed freely by the folklore of the Pacific Northwest, also known for harvests of giant trees. Voulkos's ceramics were transformed stylistically in 1952, when he made this work, after his introduction to Zen attitudes in ceramics during the visit of the Japanese potter Shoji Hamada and the British potter Bernard Leach to the Archie Bray Foundation in Helena, Montana. Realistic figurative decoration never again appeared in his work, which evolved quickly into a more abstract expressionist style.

After the Leach/Hamada visit, Rudy Autio, another Montanan long associated with the Archie Bray Foundation, expanded his use of figurative elements, eventually imbuing them with narrative power. *Three Musicians* (cat. no. 29), made about 1952, does not illustrate a specific story vignette, but it presages the vigorous animation of Autio's later vessels, which would be expressively decorated and colorfully glazed.

Folk heroes, patriotic figures, or saints whose facial features, clothing, or attributes identify them do not require the artist to place them into a complete narrative tableau. For some, their likenesses alone recall the story or stories with which they are most usually associated. In an era when facial hair was uncommon, Jesus Christ was quickly identified by his beard and robes, and George Washington's face graced every American classroom and was known to everyone who had seen a dollar bill.

The identity of some characters depends on the inclusion of specific attributes; Paul Bunyan, for example, would look like any other woodsman if not rendered in giant size or with his blue ox. Johnny Appleseed is usually depicted sowing seeds from a burlap bag, sometimes with an apple tree for clarity. Names or slogans are occasionally added as additional clues. By establishing the defining moment of a hero's aura, the act that identifies the entire story with which he or she was known becomes evident.

Farmer (1957, cat. no. 32), an enamel panel made by Joseph Trippetti, uses figures in a composition in the manner of paintings or early narrative tapestries. Enamel has never been a primary art medium in America, but this example shows Trippetti's mastery of the cloisonné technique to develop pictures suggesting story line. The work typifies the use of the vignette to define an entire story. But it is still illustration, colored very little with the artist's attitude about the story.

By the 1960s, world affairs again stimulated storytelling in craft media. Historically, the use of political and social satire or commentary is well known in the works of artists such as Honoré Daumier, William Hogarth, Toulouse-Lautrec, Francisco de Goya, Pablo Picasso, and modern-day political cartoonists. However, in the crafts or "decorative arts" (as functional handmade wares are often described), comment on political figures or situations, other than that extolling national pride, is less commonly found. The apparent social and political content in examples by Viktor Schreckengost (cat. no. 25) and Russell Barnett Aitken (cat. no. 21) is exceptional within American craft in the first half of the century.

But in the 1960s the American Dream began to tarnish, just as the artistic sophistication and technical virtuosity of America's craft makers began to flourish. Consequently, the decade saw craft makers receiving critical recognition for new work that often expressed doubts about the American ideal and larger international issues.

The freedom to experiment with abstract expressionism that Voulkos enjoyed in the 1950s found a different manifestation in the 1960s. In the decade of Pop and Op art, clay predominated over other craft media. Robert Arneson emerged as the father of what became known as the Funk Ceramics movement, which eschewed the perfection of form and surface so prized by potters. His sculptures, constructed of clay and covered with brilliant glazed color, had the look of rough spontaneity. They were provocative—a toilet just used, a typewriter with crimson fingernails where the keys should be, a toaster disgorging scorched hands—but more surreal than explicitly narrative.

As his own work moved forward into narrative self-portraits (then portraits of artists and perhaps his most famous portrait, that of murdered San Francisco mayor George Moscone), Arneson pulled a disparate group of talented Bay Area ceramists into the spotlight along with him. Richard Shaw, James Melchert, and Michael Frimkess are only a few of those who achieved recognition for their art in clay. Frimkess, in *Jumpin' at the Moon* (1968, cat. no. 37),used a classic Chinese ginger jar as a "canvas" on which he developed cartoonlike images from popular culture. Santa Claus and Uncle Sam cavort with dark-skinned women, inviting the viewer's question: are Uncle Sam and Santa Claus figures who exploit dark-skinned people for their own pleasure?

The use of visual puns, irony, and satire in ceramic art was not exclusive to California or the Bay Area, however. In Ohio, Jack Earl created an extensive body of narrative work beginning in the late 1960s. His Everyman, Bill, reappears, along with his dog, investigating the realities and puzzles of everyday existence. And in Seattle, Howard Kottler, teaching ceramics at the University of Washington, moved temporarily from making ceramics to decorating commercial plate blanks with politically provocative decal collages. *Sticks, Stones, and Bones* (1968, cat. no. 35b) combines the familiar portrait head of Abraham Lincoln with images associated with his life, death, and memorialization, but as "windows" across his face. In another work, *Peace March* (1967, cat. no. 35a), decals of pistols with legs march across the plate. In other series, Kottler used decals of famous paintings, altered for irony or humor, such as Gainsborough's *Blue Boy,* Grant Wood's *American Gothic,* and even Leonardo's *Last Supper.*

Other ceramic sculptors have borrowed from art history in diverse ways. David Gilhooley depicted scenes from Roman legend and Greek mythology, replacing humans with frogs in scenes based on the rape of the Sabine women or the story of the Trojan horse. A recurring motif in his sculpture, the frog appeared as the unlikely hero in busts of figures such as Chairman Mao and Queen Victoria; the titles of these works were often puns, too.

Though Gilhooley's frog narratives are the best known of world histories devised by ceramic sculptors, they were not singular. In Baltimore, Douglas Baldwin invented a ceramic world with ducks recreating history. Jens Art Morrison developed an entire mythical civilization with unique architectural references.

Clayton Bailey developed not only a ceramic fiction but an alternative persona as "Dr. George Gladstone: Founder, Curator of Kaolithic Curiosities" at the Wonders of the World Museum in Port Costa, California—Bailey's spoof of a fraudulent roadside tourist attraction.[2] Although the artist has produced other notable bodies of work, including water-filled buckets with bobbing, burping ceramic heads floating in them, life-size robots with blinking lights, and large rubber motorcyclists, his most complete fiction has been built around Kaolism and the Bone Age wonders he presumably has unearthed. *Bigfoot Bones* (1971, cat. no. 40) is the complete six-foot skeleton of the legendary Sasquatch of the Pacific Northwest.

Potters were experimenting with low-fire clay bodies and garish glazes, commercial decals, and molded elements attached to wheel-thrown ceramic forms, sometimes in daringly large scale. Not all the innovation was undertaken in clay, however. "Mixed media" became a new designation as an artist's medium, and constructions might include textiles knotted to driftwood or incorporate feathers or manufactured components. Jewelers and metalsmiths worked not just with metals, but integrated "found" objects into complex narrative works.

As jewelry making moved into the arena of statement and storytelling, it became less focused on precious metals and gemstones. By the 1960s jewelry had advanced from the forging and casting of stylish objects to adorn the body to the creation of miniature sculptures incorporating nontraditional materials. Robert Ebendorf, for example, used found objects along with silver and copper in *Man and His Pet Bee* (1968, cat. no. 36), an assemblage replete with sexual innuendo.

In an age when the notion of true heroes was scorned by many, the use of cartoon figures by some artists recalls Andy Warhol's appropriation of commercial and popular imagery. Superman, Little Orphan Annie, and Dick Tracy appear almost as sacred icons in a pendant by J. Fred Woell, *The Good Guys* (1966, cat. no. 34). Woell wrote of this piece, "*The Good Guys* is an attempt to say that jewelry doesn't have to be made of precious stones and metals to be valuable. I like to think that an object gets its value from what you make of it, and not of what it is made."[3]

Important persons and events continued to inspire artists, even when those who should be heroes lose the confidence of the public. Richard Nixon, for example, never won as president the popular adulation enjoyed by John F. Kennedy.

His features inspired caricature, and his term in office ended in resignation and disgrace. By the time of his presidency, the evening television news had replaced fiction and history as the fodder for artistic storytelling. War, once the stuff of heroes and flag waving, was transformed by the nightly news from Southeast Asia into chilling human tragedy.

The antiwar, antiestablishment, and antigovernment sentiments of the 1960s offered new subject matter for appropriation and interpretation. Television, magazine, and newspaper reporting were digested and focused by a number of artists. Helena Hernmarck's *Talking Trudeau-Nixon* (1969, cat. no. 38) resulted from the weaver's interest in newsreels and the black-and-white dot pattern of newsprint. She says of the piece, "The idea with the boy was that he was the victim of the decisions of the politicians and he looked us straight in the eye— the others talked at each other."[4] With the dramatic impact of a news broadcast, the tapestry introduced photorealism, then popular in painting, into textiles. The work was exhibited in Lausanne, Switzerland, in one of the first international tapestry biennial exhibitions. Although the biennials were expected to revive interest in pictorial tapestry, Hernmarck's piece was one of the few exhibited, as the series went on to favor sculptural textile constructions. Narrative tapestries were not to win prominence in the twentieth century.

New patterning techniques brought storytelling to textiles in the 1970s. Woven textiles, pictorial or not, were eclipsed by an interest in the textile surface. Traditional Asian dyeing processes such as ikat, plangi, and batik joined such contemporary technical processes as color photocopying and heat-transfer printing to decorate fabric. Embroidery, beadwork, new forms of quilt making, and nontraditional materials like videotape and motion picture film became part of the artistic toolbox of fiber artists, as they were now called. Another new term, wearable art, described the possibilities of adapting textile decoration and clothing structure into an innovative hybrid. The results ranged from clothing of classic simplicity, but with bold surface embellishments, to theatrical garments more suited to display than wear.

Ed Rossbach, respected for his exploration of creative possibilities of structural textile techniques, constructed *Handgun* (1975, cat. no. 45) of plaited paper. The artist says, "Someone painted a graffiti handgun on the stairs of the building where I worked. You stepped on it when you entered the building. Before it disappeared, I photographed it and used the Xeroxed image on a bark basket. My plaited handgun was inspired, rather indirectly, by the Robert Kennedy assassination. A small photograph of the gun was in a newspaper that was lying around on my work table for quite a while. In time I recognized it as an image that I wanted to use."[5] This starkly minimal image distills the essence of violence; the vibrant red, suggesting blood, contrasts sharply with the purity of the white background, boldly reminding us of the criminal act that robbed the country of a promising leader. Rossbach has continued to mine the news for events and personalities for his graphic images. Film actor John Travolta, baseball star Pete Rose, and former astronaut John Glenn have all been the subject of his work over the years.

Although Rossbach has used heat-transfer to print color photocopies onto fabric, it is his wife, Katherine Westphal, who has truly exploited such modern technology as an artist's tool. Her *New Treasures of Tutankhamen* (1977–78, cat. no. 48) was influenced by a trip to Egypt in which the artist found the old Egypt she knew to have been overwhelmed by the trappings and souvenirs of the tourist industry. Both universal and personal, Westphal's art combines such easily recognized icons as the pyramids and the Sphinx with informal photographs of travelers. The artist says that she "tried to make the connections between the tourists, the old treasures, and myths. The images are derived from my sketchbook and my camera. Images in museums, at sites, of camels, of tourists, just the whole hodge-podge of Egypt as I experienced it. The borders are ushabti figures, the small blue faience sculptures all packed into painted boxes and displayed in the museum in Cairo. The central portion is a fantasy world of overlapping forms all emerging from the desert sands."[6] The panne velvet cushions, quilts, dalmatics, and scrolls in this body of Westphal's work recall as well the treasures from Tutankhamen's tomb, the subject of stylistic revivals several times in the past.

Joan Steiner, like Westphal, has externalized her own life as the subject of much of her wearable art, depicting in vests the bathroom, furnace room, kitchen, and front porch of her house. She also uses photographs, but as inspiration and detail information as she painstakingly develops each "portrait" in stitched and stuffed fabric. She says of *Manhattan Collar* (1979, cat. no. 52), "I used a tremendous amount of photographic reference—primarily souvenir booklets about NYC. I like the fact that the collar zips down Fifth Avenue. The piece originally included two tiny helicopter earrings which may or may not have gotten lost along the way."[7] New York here is presented as an icon, its famous Chrysler and Empire State buildings readily identified, evoking for each viewer his or her own references to the Big Apple, whether inspired by real life or the movies.

The American flag was the country's first political narrative textile and remains its most famous. Its stars representing the fifty states and its stripes the original thirteen colonies, the flag has potent symbolism for Americans. Its use in art, found to be disrespectful by many patriotic Americans, recently has been the subject of much public controversy.

Arturo Alonzo Sandoval has for some time examined the American flag as a symbol of patriotism and a vehicle for social comment. A Hispanic-American descended from weavers in New Mexico, he is well aware of our nation's avowed embrace of immigrants, and its unkept promises. Becoming concerned about the rise in unemployment, poverty, and distrust of the government during the Reagan era, Sandoval sought an image that would relate to and motivate the common man. He began a series titled State of the Union and used the American flag as its central image. Although familiar with prior use of the flag in antiwar and political art and in Pop art, he was drawn to this symbol "to communicate my innermost feelings of frustration and disgust, my passion and ideals, my humanness and sensitivity."[8] State of the Union No. 10—Lady Liberty's Centennial Celebration (1987, cat. no. 65) was created as a narrative on the issue of freedom as represented by the Statue of Liberty. The piece was only the second that Sandoval had created in silk, and the artist found "the physical experience of handling all that silk was fabulous. I felt as if I was making Lady Liberty a wedding dress."[9]

Political art and art that comments on social issues have become important aspects of American freedom of speech. Sandoval's other flag images are less benign than this work, which was made for an international traveling exhibition of American fiber art sponsored by the U.S. government. Other artists have also produced politically provocative narratives in craft media. Joyce J. Scott has often commented on racial and political issues in her performance art, beadwork assemblage necklaces, and sculpture, alluding to physical abuse and violence, and even the subtle discrimination against fat people. In Eaten Alive: South Africa's Greatest Fear (1986, cat. no. 61), she graphically depicts in three dimensions her abhorrence of apartheid, racism, and sexism.

Bruce Metcalf's brooch, A Present from the Government (1989, cat. no. 70), is fairly typical of the artist's jewelry. The figure with an oversized head is an Everyman, who stands threatened by a menacing bundle of missiles, implements of destruction. Metcalf comments, "He should have known better—after all, our taxes contribute to [military] production . . . —but still, the fellow seems distressed. It's a gift he does not welcome. . . . I think most people would understand the pin to be antimilitaristic."[10]

Antimilitarism has been a strong force in narrative craft in the twentieth century, from Viktor Schreckengost's Apocalypse '42 (cat. no. 25) caricaturing the enemies in World War II, to Paul Marioni's Hiroshima (1988, cat. no. 68). Marioni values ambiguity in the meaning of his art, but in this sculpture he leaves no doubt about his dread of nuclear destruction, the full horror of which he began to understand after attending a peace ceremony in Hiroshima on August 6, 1984. He recaptured that horror in the face he created in Hiroshima. Inlaid glass eyes and realistic teeth are set into a horribly distorted, cast glass face. The artist has said, "The viewer realizes that this is not a cartoon or a characterization of a human face. This is a horribly disfigured human being."[11] The unblinking, staring eyes seem to follow the viewer around the room, demanding that you consider the human cost of nuclear arms.

Richard Notkin was a student of Robert Arneson's at the University of California at Davis during the heyday of the Funk Ceramics movement. Arneson has sometimes created sculpture to protest the proliferation of nuclear arms and the destruction of war; Notkin has nearly always used his talents to record in clay his social and political concerns. Unlike ceramists associated with the funk movement, however, Notkin's work is not only carefully developed intellectually, it is meticulously made. Funk ceramists produced one-liners; Notkin creates treatises.

In *Vain Imaginings* (1978, cat. no. 49), the symbol of death/evil, a skull—a recurring motif in Notkin's work—apparently watches another skull on a television screen. One leg of the table forming the stage for this tableau has not been completely cut from a tree trunk, perhaps symbolizing man's use, or misuse, of nature. A chess set denoting the consequences of human decisions (or "plays") is, like the skull, a recurring symbol in Notkin's sculpture. This piece predates the much-published *Universal Hostage Crisis* (1981), which more overtly commented on the "big button" that can trigger a war and the detonation of the atomic bomb over Hiroshima. Notkin's exacting workmanship, in service to his highly intellectualized, abstracted realism, is unmatched in American ceramics. Subsequent series—especially the unglazed Yixing-style teapots, many modeled after nuclear cooling towers with skull-shaped clouds—have been powerful statements about the consequences of human decisions.

Terrie Hancock Mangat's *Desert Storm* (1991, cat. no. 72) and Alan Stirt's *War Bowl* (1991, cat. no. 73) together express Americans' differing feelings about war. Mangat's pieced quilt of missiles tied with ribbons reminds us of trees tied with yellow ribbons—symbols at home welcoming loved ones back from war—and of instruments of destruction. Tiny automobiles, skeletons, and gas pumps symbolize the human toll of a war waged to keep affordable gas flowing to American cars from sources in the Middle East. Stirt's charred turned-wood bowl, suggestive of the devastation of bombing, also was made in response to the Gulf War and the propaganda assault on the American public. Stirt has written, "In the midst of all the talk and flag waving there seemed to be almost no acknowledgment of the destructive aspects of the war. The assault was not only against people and objects but against the human spirit itself. The motivation to make this bowl was to exorcise my own fears and confusion."[12]

Personal narratives expressed in public art characterize the diversity of storytelling in American craft. Human response to such large issues as war and social change will perhaps always remain among the most strongly felt narratives in art, however personal or diversely depicted. The universal values of love, family, country, and religion shared by people of many nations are strong sources of inspiration. The humans that we imbue with such virtues become embodiments of shared beliefs, or icons.

Kiff Slemmons, like J. Fred Woell (cat. no. 34), wishing for real-life men and women—rather than comic book characters—to call heroes, in 1987 embarked on a series of thirty-five brooches called Hands of the Heroes (cat. no. 66). Thinking of the loss of heroes in our culture to replacement by celebrities, Slemmons com-memorated her own heroes, exploring her theme by using the image of the hand as a base or stage. Slemmons says, "The hand is a familiar and strong image in the jewelry of many cultures, past and present. Each hand in this series con-tains personal attributes of specific people who exemplify the idea of hero in some way."[13] Slemmons's examination of her own childhood idols and ideals is characteristic of narrative craft of the 1980s. Our fears, phobias, memories, and aspirations may all be woven into the textures and graphics of storytelling art.

Judy Jensen found inspiration for *Denial* (1988, cat. no. 67) while listening to instructions about the use of emergency flotation devices on an airplane flight. She particularly responded to the images depicted in the safety brochure of crash procedures. "As a nation of idealists," says Jensen, "I feel that most Americans maintain their sense of idealism about our country by denying the inherent harm in many aspects of American life and politics, even when continually confronted with evidence to the contrary."[14]

Jan Holcomb creates surrealistic "dimensional paintings" in stoneware. A self-taught artist, he has drawn cartoonlike images—especially faces—since childhood. The face and human image have become the catalyst and center for his narrative situations. *Two Worlds* (1987, cat. no. 63) was inspired by a figure doing a handstand; from it the artist developed a psychological landscape that is both evocative and suggestive. Although Holcomb had a specific narrative in mind, he prefers to leave the piece open to interpretation.[15] Like other of his tableaux, *Two Worlds* suggests isolation, and perhaps despair, which viewers have sometimes associated with the artist's struggle against multiple sclerosis.

More admittedly personal is Martha Banyas's *Testimony* (1979, cat. no. 50), which the artist made at the end of a long and difficult relationship. According to Banyas, "Another person became involved, and soon it was the end—indicated by the double arms . . . 'I want this, but I also want that.' . . . I decided to use art for my own purpose and [made] a piece to purge the pain. The parrot is me. The landscape is that inner landscape we created when together. The incredible beauty, danger, and pain is all wrapped up into this piece—and it worked its healing."[16]

Pain and healing of another sort inspired Michael Aschenbrenner's *22nd Sur-gical* (1981, cat. no. 53), which stems from his convalescence in a military hospital during the Vietnam War. The piece recalls how the artist injured his knee jump-ing from a helicopter and had to walk on his bad leg for two weeks before being rescued. One of the earliest in a series of mixed-media works based on this inci-dent, the work incorporates a glass leg bone that resembles a rifle, with a cable maintaining tension between the bandaged end (the butt) and the barrel. The glass limb is displayed like "exhibit A" against a white and deep blue-black painting that is abstract but for a crudely drawn handsaw and a spread-eagled stick figure on a table with a red arrow pointing to the right knee. Later works in the series did away with the painting and emphasized bandaged glass bones, sometimes installed on a wall in a group. The fragility of the sparkling, beautiful glass limb represented amidst the ugliness of war evokes pungent memories in those with related experiences.[17]

Dana Boussard's fusion of technique and complex imagery is typical of storytelling—and craft—in the 1980s. After living in Chicago, New York, and San Francisco, she returned as a mature artist to her home state of Montana. Her love of the West has supplied both the subject matter and style of her art, which reminds one of Plains Indian buffalo-hide paintings. *We Met with Oh, Such Separate Dreams* (1987, cat. no. 62) is a portrait piece of her husband, Stan Reifel, herself, and the horses that dominate their sixty acres. When Reifel decided to acquire horses against Boussard's better judgment, the artist took refuge in her work. Boussard says, "On the right side, Stan hovers, inextricably tied to the land and animals. On the other side is a portrait of me, floating high and aloof, separated by barbs, wanting very little to do with the venture. Yet in spite of it all, we remain tied together in our lives."[18]

Boussard, who earned degrees in drawing, painting, and printmaking, found that she prefers not to rely rigorously and exclusively on a single medium. Today her fiber constructions blend airbrushed painting on fabric with appliqué, direct painting, and embroidery. This diversity of process exemplifies the freedom craft artists have enjoyed since the dawning of the Surface Design movement in the 1970s.

Storytelling is often well suited to large-scale corporate and public commissions, particularly the "percent-for-art" programs that began in the 1970s. Historical themes or those with regional specificity are often favored by the selection committees for such commissions. Dana Boussard has made a number of large wall hangings for airports and municipal buildings. Richard Posner, whose leaded-glass panels of the 1970s showed his promise as a storyteller, also has found public art to be an important aspect of his oeuvre. His mixed-media art has been commissioned for such diverse buildings as a science museum, county elections building, veterans' medical center, university hospital, baseball stadium, criminal justice center, municipal airport, water sewage treatment plant, and a district office of the U.S. Food and Drug Administration.

Since his installation of *The Dream Chartres of Four Gone Conclusions* (1976–78) at the Exploratorium in San Francisco, Posner has continued to wed literary and historical references, in words and images, to the place and purpose of his commissions.

Although it is difficult to typify a Posner installation, except perhaps through his use of puns, quotes, and sometimes corny titles, *The Crystal Pallets: deFence of Light* (1983, fig. 1) may serve as a point of discussion. Installed between the inner and outer glass window panes of the Multnomah County Elections Building in Portland, Oregon—from where it is visible from both the street and the

Fig. 1. Richard Posner, *The Crystal Pallets: deFence of Light* (detail), 1983, Multnomah County Elections Building, Portland, Oregon.

Fig. 2. *AIDS Memorial Quilt*, Names Project, displayed in Washington, D.C., 1988. Photo: Marcel Miranda III.

visitors' lobby—the work extends for fifty feet across the renovated one-story building. Symbols and aphorisms referring to the American political process and American history are posted on a glass picket fence. The silhouettes of animals familiar in political allegory—the lame duck and the dark horse—are combined with photo-etched placards, photographs, slogans, and inscriptions relating to the democratic process and political topics of local importance. Broken bottles at the bottom of the fence allude to the fragility of the political system and the need for vigilant maintenance. "I decided to make the work an 'electoral collage,'" Posner has said, playing with words in his customary way, "that was political both by intention and consequence. It illuminates the fence-mending rituals of Jeffersonian democracy."[19] Posner stands alone in his total integration of the "story" of his commissioned art with its iconography and text.

The term "large scale" has new meaning when referring to the immense quilt commemorating some of the one million persons who have died worldwide in the AIDS epidemic. The Names Project was founded to encourage friends, families, and loved ones to remember those who perished from the disease by making quilt panels incorporating personal emblems. In 1988 in Washington, D.C., the three-by-six-foot quilt squares were spread side by side—covering the equivalent of eight football fields—across the green expanse of the Ellipse. They were an unforgettable reminder, to more than two-and-one-half-million visitors, of individuals, their occupations, hobbies, loves, and lives (fig. 2). As deaths from AIDS mount, the twenty-one thousand panels that now constitute the quilt are too many to be exhibited in one place, and state AIDS quilts have begun to appear.

Because the first victims of the disease in the United States were homosexual men, popular and government support for aggressive research and appropriate health care was slow in coming. In a subtle way the quilt does not stress AIDS as a "gay" disease but emphasizes the universal sense of loss felt for any human life. It is the contemporary equivalent of a nineteenth-century friendship quilt, made enormous in scale, not by professional artists but by the loving hands of talented amateurs.

The quilt format regained popularity among contemporary artists when the Surface Design movement offered to quilt makers such unorthodox patterning techniques as direct dyeing and painting on fabric, rubber stamping of motifs, and integration of unconventional materials and found objects. African-American artists such as Faith Ringgold have found an artistic antecedent for their work in quilts made by African slaves in America and their descendants. Ringgold, like Betye Saar, Alison Saar, and Joyce J. Scott, has called on her experiences as a black woman in America to shape her art. Her quilts, and the dolls that she has also made, sometimes illustrate her recollections of family history and sometimes visually record hypothetical meetings of historical figures. Such quilts—actually soft paintings—force us to examine the exclusion from mainstream history of the accomplishments of women, especially black women.

Such portraiture is hardly new to painting traditions, but it has become more notable in art made with craft materials and methods, despite the tradition of Bible quilts and friendship quilts in the last century. Judy Chicago's epic mixed-media sculptural installation completed in 1979, *The Dinner Party* (fig. 3), literally took symbolism as portraiture to a new dimension. Like a traditional pieced-quilt completed by women at a quilting bee, *The Dinner Party* was a group effort of some four hundred ceramists, china painters, and needleworkers. Each of thirty-nine place settings at a triangular table, forty-eight feet on each side, depicts a famous woman in the history of the Western world. The table rests on a tile floor inscribed with the names of some 999 additional women of achievement.

Chicago has described the work as "a reinterpretation of The Last Supper. I thought 'men had a Last Supper, but women have had dinner parties.' (Moreover, it was probably women who cooked the food for that famous Last Supper.) . . . The use of china painting and needlework—examples of women's traditional arts—suggests that in our cultural myopia about 'women's work,' we have deprived ourselves of the rich products, not only of women's culture, but also of women's minds and energies."[20]

The Dinner Party attracted blockbuster audiences in the six countries where it was shown but was often derided as pornography by those who could not see beyond vagina forms in the butterfly and flower abstractions on many of the plates. Such controversy undoubtedly helped to increase attendance, and some who came to see it perhaps took the time to understand the complex narrative imagery and symbolism in each of the unique place settings.

A mythical gathering of artists is also the subject of Patti Warashina's masterful ceramic sculpture, *'A' Procession* (1985, fig. 4), commissioned by the Seattle Art Commission for permanent installation in the city's Opera House. For this work—appropriately operatic in concept and execution—the artist created miniature full-body portraits of seventy-one leading figures in Seattle's contemporary art establishment in a gleeful procession crossing a ten-foot bridge. The bridge's arch, and the bony white of the porcelain figures, suggests a frieze on a Greek pediment. But this is no dignified tableau; these are wildly animated artists brandishing the tools of their professions—pens, paintbrushes, film. The spirit of the piece is the joy of art—making or experiencing it.

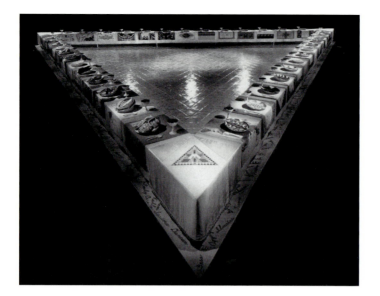 

Fig. 3. Judy Chicago, *The Dinner Party*, 1979, mixed media, 48 × 48 × 48 ft. © Judy Chicago 1979. Photo: Donald Woodman.

Fig. 4. Patti Warashina, '*A' Procession* (detail), 1985, porcelain. Photo: Roger Schreiber.

Influenced by the Funk Ceramics movement in the 1960s, Warashina studied ceramics with Howard Kottler at the University of Washington. Her mastery of ceramic techniques and the deftness of her drawing and painting skills enable her to comment visually, and with apparent ease, on her own life and the ironies of modern times. *Mother Goosed* (1974, cat. no. 42) combines Warashina's recurring references to the roles of modern woman with myth and folk tales, here evoking Leda and the Swan and Mother Goose. A suburban housewife seems trapped in a box (an oven or washing machine, or a love nest with a heart-shaped door?) with a goose (a modern version of the swan who makes love to Leda?). Is she trapped by a symbol of housework, unable to escape, or willing to succumb to dreamlike romance? Such surrealist imagery is not new to Warashina, whose sculpture had evolved by the 1980s into tabletop vignettes of female figures confronting the symbols of housewifery and motherhood.

Warashina is only one of several former Kottler students who have adopted storytelling imagery. Michael Lucero, Nancy Carman, Margaret Ford, and Mark Burns continue to use the human figure in personal, and surreal, ways. Burns, who has redefined several of the pantheon of Catholic saints in a modern context, alludes in *Saint Vitus* (1983, cat. no. 59) to the patron saint of artists, musicians, and performers, and to the medieval disease, Saint Vitus's dance, that caused its victims literally to twitch themselves to death. The artist reinvented the saint according to pop culture, with the "victims" now the convulsive dancers of contemporary punk nightclubs. Saint Vitus, cast in the artist's features, is dressed in black leather; his talisman is rock 'n' roll, represented by a radio, the "altar of the airwaves."[21]

Surrealism, often characterized by dreamlike compositions of seemingly unrelated images, is increasingly apparent in the narrative story lines of craft artists. Thomas Lundberg, in his embroidered miniature picture *Dog in the Water* (1981, cat. no. 55), uses everyday life as a starting point. His objects "are time markers, grounded in particular locations and momentary light conditions. These pictures are sparked by things I see, but are not exact diary entries. Rather, my work is like a story or a dream, where images pulled from the stream of events are isolated and given a new life. These pictures use small details and glimpses of life to reflect larger cycles and the bigger, mysterious world."[22] With needle and thread, Lundberg manipulates light and dark, color and image, creating enigmatic juxtapositions of real and imagined elements.

David Furman cast his dog, Molly, as the solo star in a series of miniature ceramic interiors made in the 1970s, among them *In the Boudoir with Molly, In the Den with Molly, Molly on the ¾ Couch,* and *Molly Resting.* More portraiture —of place and pet—than surreal tableau, *In the Bathroom with Molly* (1975, cat. no. 44) is typical of Furman's straightforward rendering of a familiar interior populated only by Molly, his first pet and singular model. "In my work I have been preoccupied with the reflective and reflexive ideas and emotions I have about space, landscape, and sense of place. Manifest in those ideas are thoughts and problems of scale change, the ability to exceed one's physical limitations, and the creations of man. I see my house as a second skin, reflective of me in a unique and personal way. I strive to reflect in my work a personal and personable quality. I want to reveal, share, and whisper secrets. Enter into my work Molly, the dog. She is my emissary—she is a model I work from in a classical manner, and she is much more."[23]

Furman, like Warashina and others, works in a relatively small scale that recalls porcelain figurines of the eighteenth century. Still popular today, such figurines are production-line popular art depicting characters familiar from children's stories, history, and mythology. Like Rogers groups of the nineteenth century (plaster production statuary depicting homely scenes of courtship, marriage, and family life) and Norman Rockwell's *Saturday Evening Post* covers, they capture story line in a frozen moment that, by association and familiarity, allows us to imagine an entire narrative.

Other artists have similarly distilled a moment and, with minimal clues, made the viewer guess the plot. Wendell Castle, respected for his organic sculptural furniture, for a brief period in the 1970s began to make furniture with sculptural anecdotes as the principal element. A carved leather jacket hangs from the back of a carved-wood chair; a coatrack sports a carved topcoat. *Table with Gloves and Keys* (1981, cat. no. 54) suggests a room that someone has just exited, leaving behind a personal item, a clue, from which the viewer might construct a story about the owner and the circumstances in which the items were left behind.

Narrative and craft have changed since World War II. As examples in this catalogue demonstrate, storytelling can be global or personal, about love or war, terror or joy. Artists working in a narrative format may tell a story with one or more "moments" that are critical to its plot, or they may reduce imagery to purely symbolic images and colors. Craft, no longer exclusively functional, has become diverse in media and in the application of time-honored techniques. Clay is not just for thrown pots but slip-cast teapots and gigantic hand-built sculpture. Metals other than silver and gold are used in contemporary jewelry, and forms previously considered merely decorative, such as forged weather vanes or architectural ornament, now are considered large-scale works of art. Wood, in furniture and turned bowls, has emerged as an expressive material suited not only for carved sculpture. Textiles have, in the diversity of dyeing and patterning methods as well as woven imagery, retained their place in the history of narrative art. And, finally, glass has emerged in the past thirty years as a startling "new" material employed by contemporary artists for more than its crystalline beauty. Narrative is everywhere, and can be interpreted in every medium.

NOTES

1. Lenore Tawney, letter to author, July 1992.
2. Clayton Bailey, letter to author, July 27, 1992, accompanied by *Wonders of the World Museum, Catalog of Kaolithic Curiosities and Scientific Wonders,* and miscellaneous press clippings.
3. Lee Nordness, *Objects: USA* (New York: Viking Press, 1970), p. 226.
4. Helena Hernmarck, statement by the artist, February 5, 1990, file copy, American Craft Museum, New York.
5. Ed Rossbach, artist's statement to author, August 9, 1992.
6. Katherine Westphal, artist's statement to author, August 6, 1992.
7. Joan Steiner, letter to author, August 4, 1992.
8. Arturo Alonzo Sandoval, letter to author, July 27, 1992, accompanied by 1986 statements on the creation of the State of the Union series.
9. Ibid.
10. Bruce Metcalf, letter to author, July 27, 1992.
11. Paul Marioni, letter to author, July 30, 1992.
12. Alan Stirt, letter to author, July 28, 1992.
13. Kiff Slemmons, artist's statement to author, September 22, 1991.
14. Judy Jensen, artist's statement to author, July 22, 1992.
15. Jan Holcomb, letter to author, July 1992.
16. Martha Banyas, letter to author, August 12, 1992.
17. John Perreault, "Michael Aschenbrenner: Glass Plus," *Glass,* no. 40 (Spring/Summer 1990), p. 28.
18. Dana Boussard, letter to author, August 6, 1992.
19. Ron Glowen, "Glass Encounters: Richard Posner," *American Craft* 44, no. 3 (June/July 1984), p. 46.
20. Judy Chicago, "The Dinner Party Project," *The Dinner Party: Judy Chicago* (San Francisco: San Francisco Museum of Modern Art, 1979), p. 3.
21. Mark Burns, letter to author, August 18, 1992.
22. Tom Lundberg, artist's statement, 1988–89, author's collection.
23. David Furman, artist's statement, 1974, author's collection.

CATALOGUE

1. *MUSIC FOLDER COVER*
   EARLY 20TH CENTURY

   SYDNEY RICHMOND BURLEIGH
2. *KING ARTHUR CHEST*
   CA. 1900

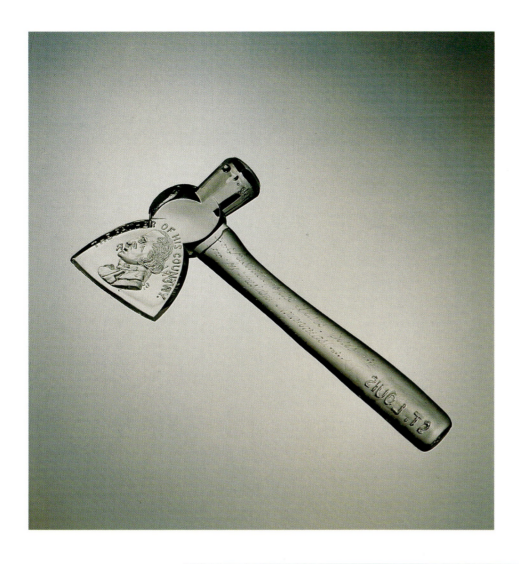

3. *HATCHET*
    1904

4. *TABLE MAT*
    CA. 1905

ARTHUR FRANCIS MATHEWS AND LUCIA KLEINHANS MATHEWS

5. *DROP-FRONT DESK*

CA. 1906–15

6. QUILT

1907–1908

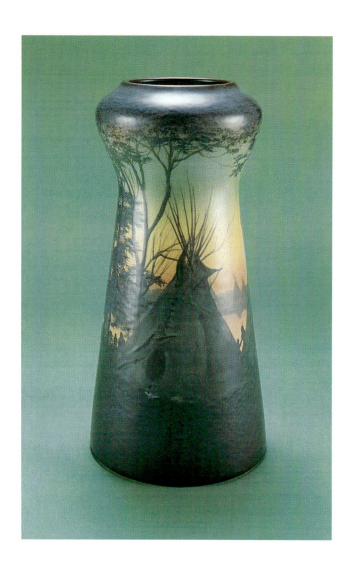

EDWARD T. HURLEY

7. ROOKWOOD VASE

CA. 1909

8. VICTORY—1918

1918

BENIAMINO B. BUFANO

9. *CHINESE MAN AND WOMAN*

1921

10. *PLAQUE*

CA. 1924–30

ARTHUR B. DAVIES
11. *AT THE GATES OF MORNING*
CA. 1925

RENÉ CLARKE
12. *STADIUM*
1927

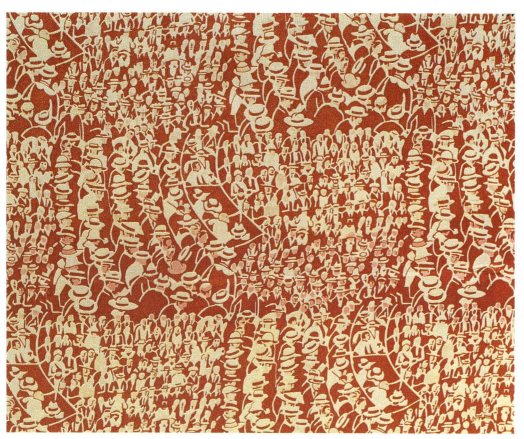

JOHN HELD, JR.

13. *RHAPSODY*

1927

VICTOR F. VON LOSSBERG

14. *AMERICA*

1927

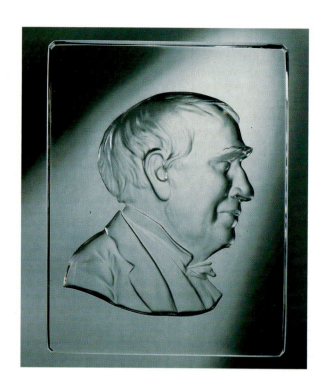

FREDERICK CARDER

15. *COMMEMORATIVE PLAQUE WITH INTAGLIO*
    PORTRAIT OF THOMAS ALVA EDISON
    1929

LILLIAN HOLM

16. *FIRST SIGHT OF NEW YORK*
    EARLY 1930S

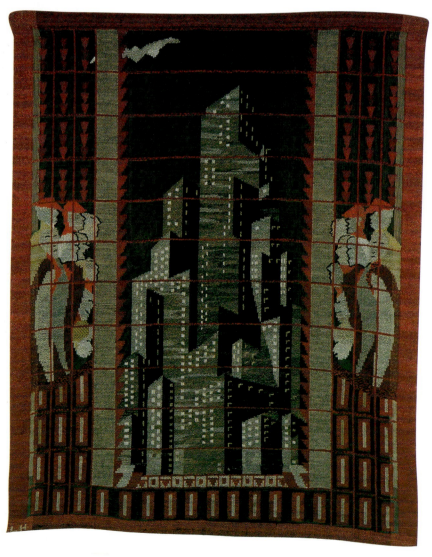

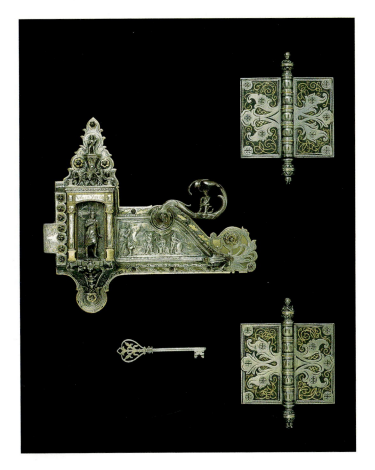

FRANK L. KORALEWSKY

17. *LOCK WITH HINGES AND KEY*

1932

HENRY VARNUM POOR

18. *TEN NIGHTS IN A BAR ROOM*

1932

ELIEL AND LOJA SAARINEN

19. *SAMPLE FOR THE FESTIVAL OF*
THE MAY QUEEN HANGING
1932

BERTHA STENGE
20. *CENTURY OF PROGRESS QUILT*
1933

RUSSELL BARNETT AITKEN
21. *FUTILITY OF A WELL-ORDERED LIFE*
1935

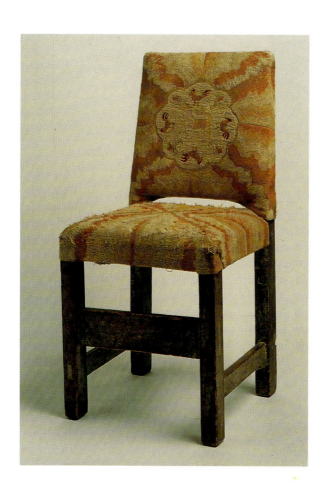

DOMINGO TEJADA

22. *CHAIR WITH EMBROIDERED COVER*

1937

EDRIS ECKHARDT

23. *EARTH*

1939

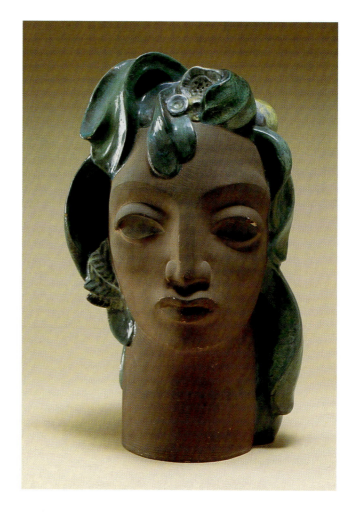

ARTHUR NEVILL KIRK
24. *TRIPTYCH WITH VIRGIN AND CHILD*
CA. 1940

VIKTOR SCHRECKENGOST
25. *APOCALYPSE '42*
1942

SIDNEY WAUGH
26. *THE BOWL OF AMERICAN LEGENDS*
    1942

THOMAS MCCLURE
27. *CARVED BOWL (PASSION OF CHRIST)*
    1947

EDWIN AND MARY SCHEIER
28. *JUDGMENT OF SOLOMON*
1948

RUDY AUTIO
29. *THREE MUSICIANS*
CA. 1952

PETER VOULKOS

30. *BABE, THE BLUE OX*

CA. 1952

LENORE TAWNEY

31. *BOUND MAN*

1957

JOSEPH TRIPPETTI
32. *FARMER*
1957

TOMMY SIMPSON
33. *FLOWER GARDEN*
1965

J. FRED WOELL

34. *THE GOOD GUYS*

1966

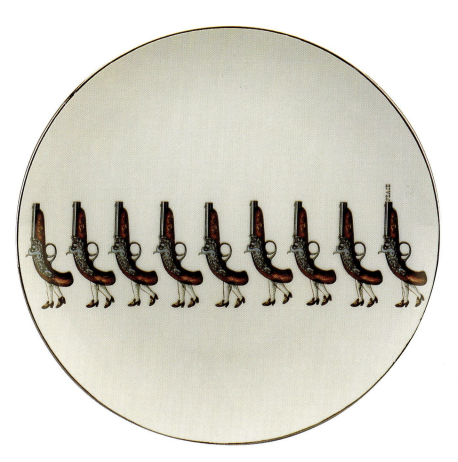

HOWARD KOTTLER
35A. *PEACE MARCH*
1967

HOWARD KOTTLER
35B. *STICKS, STONES, AND BONES*
1968

ROBERT EBENDORF
36. *MAN AND HIS PET BEE*
1968

MICHAEL FRIMKESS
37. *JUMPIN' AT THE MOON*
1968

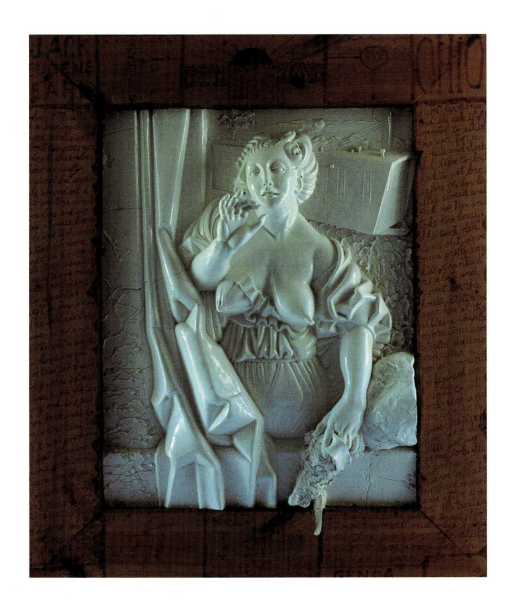

HELENA HERNMARCK

38. *TALKING TRUDEAU-NIXON*

1969

JACK EARL

39. *UNTITLED*

1969–70

CLAYTON BAILEY
40. *BIGFOOT BONES*
1971

ELEANOR MOTY
41. *DUAL IMAGE PIN*
1974

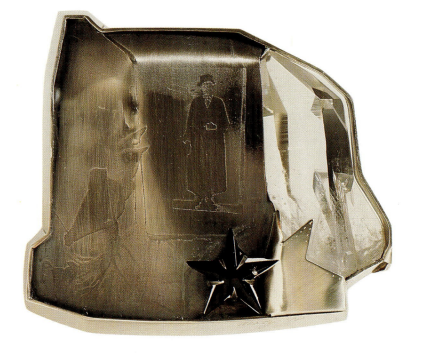

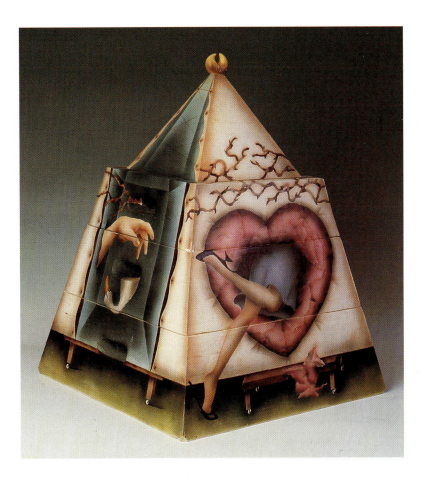

PATTI WARASHINA
42. *MOTHER GOOSED*
1974

VIOLA FREY
43. *JUNKYARD DREAMING*
1975

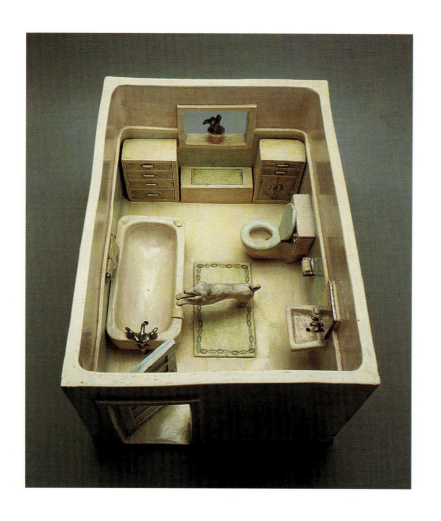

DAVID FURMAN
44. *IN THE BATHROOM WITH MOLLY*
1975

ED ROSSBACH
45. *HANDGUN*
1975

JIM COTTER

46. *TEXAS DOUBLE DIPPER*

1976

MARTHA GLOWACKI

47. *OVERLOOKING WELLS, JUNE, 1977*

1977

KATHERINE WESTPHAL

48. *NEW TREASURES OF TUTANKHAMEN* (DETAIL)
1977–78

RICHARD NOTKIN

49. *VAIN IMAGININGS*
1978

MARTHA BANYAS
50. *TESTIMONY*
1979

AUDREY HANDLER
51. *AN AMERICAN BREAKFAST*
1979
(NOT ILLUSTRATED)

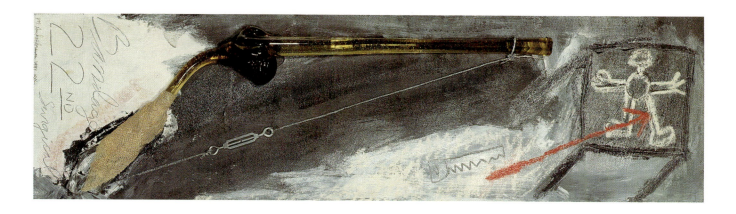

JOAN STEINER

52. *MANHATTAN COLLAR*

1979

MICHAEL ASCHENBRENNER

53. *22ND SURGICAL*

1981

WENDELL CASTLE

54. *TABLE WITH GLOVES AND KEYS*

1981

THOMAS LUNDBERG

55. *DOG IN THE WATER*

1981

ESTHER LUTTIKHUIZEN

56. *SPRATS*

1981

RICKY BERNSTEIN

57. *IT'S TIME TO GET UP!*

1982

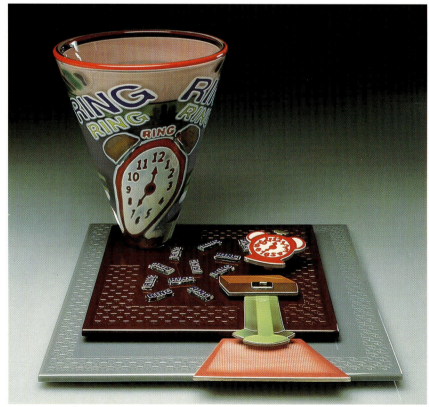

KENNETH FERGUSON

58. *PLATTER WITH ADAM AND EVE*

1982

MARK BURNS

59. *SAINT VITUS*

1983

D. R. WAGNER

60. *THE FINGERING*

1984

JOYCE J. SCOTT

61. *EATEN ALIVE: SOUTH AFRICA'S*
GREATEST FEAR

1986

DANA BOUSSARD

62. *WE MET WITH OH, SUCH SEPARATE DREAMS*

1987

JAN HOLCOMB

63. *TWO WORLDS*

1987

GERHARDT KNODEL

64. *GUARDIANS OF THE NEW DAY*

1987

ARTURO ALONZO SANDOVAL

65. *STATE OF THE UNION NO. 10—LADY LIBERTY'S CENTENNIAL CELEBRATION*

1987

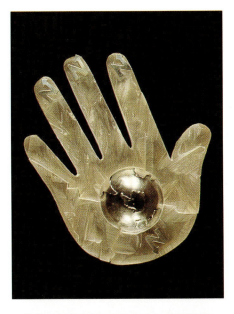

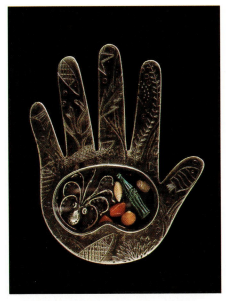

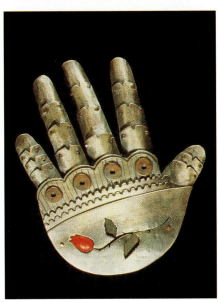

LEFT TO RIGHT:

KIFF SLEMMONS

66A. *ROALD AMUNDSEN*
1987

66B. *JACQUES COUSTEAU*
1988

66C. *EMILY DICKINSON*
1988

66D. *HOUDINI*
1987

66E. *DON QUIXOTE*
1989

JUDY JENSEN
67. *DENIAL*
1988

PAUL MARIONI
68. *HIROSHIMA*
1988

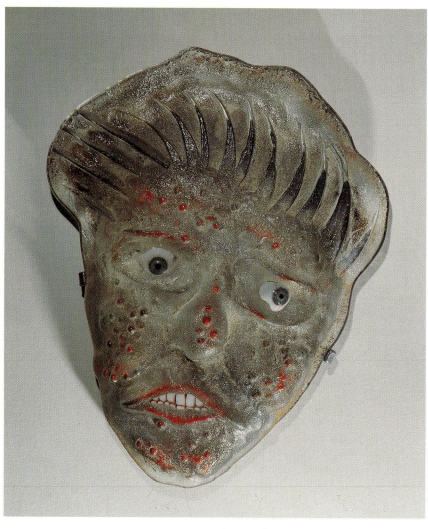

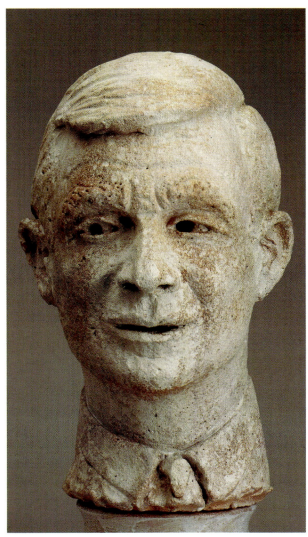

ROBERT ARNESON
69A. *CHIEF EXECUTIVE OFFICER*
1989

ROBERT ARNESON
69B. *RAPIST AND DRUG DEALER*
1989

BRUCE METCALF
70. *A PRESENT FROM THE GOVERNMENT*
1989

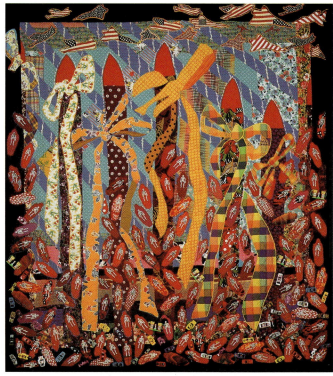

RONNA NEUENSCHWANDER

71. *N'NA AND HER CAN*

1990

TERRIE HANCOCK MANGAT

72. *DESERT STORM*

1991

ALAN STIRT

73. *WAR BOWL*

1991

CHECKLIST

Height precedes width precedes depth.

1. *Music Folder Cover*, early 20th century
Edward F. Caldwell and Company, maker
Enamel on copper attached to leather
folder
17½ × 14 × 1¾ in. (with support)
Cranbrook Educational Community,
Cranbrook House, Michigan, CEC-297

2. Sydney Richmond Burleigh
King Arthur Chest, ca. 1900
Julia Lippitt Mauran, carver
Carved and painted oak
21¾ × 40 × 21⅞ in.
Museum of Art, Rhode Island School of
Design, Providence, bequest of Isaac C.
Bates, 13.429

3. *Hatchet*, 1904
Libbey Glass Company, Toledo, Ohio,
maker
Colorless glass, pressed and engraved
7⅞ × 4⅛ in.
Corning Museum of Glass, Corning, New
York, gift of J. M. Hutchinson, 81.4.130

4. *Table Mat*, ca. 1905
Sybil Carter Indian Lace Association,
Oneida Indian reservation, Wisconsin
Linen, bobbin-made lace inserts and
edging on plain-weave
12½ × 17 in.
Cooper-Hewitt National Museum of
Design, Smithsonian Institution, New
York, gift of Mrs. Bayard Cutting in
memory of Miss Mary Parsons, 1943-44-5

5. Arthur Francis Mathews and Lucia
Kleinhans Mathews
Drop-Front Desk, ca. 1906–15
Oak or maple and rosewood, carved and
painted, with metal fittings
57⅛ × 47⅞ × 20 in. (closed)
Oakland Museum, California, gift of the
Concours d'Antiques, Art Guild, 72.8.5

6. *Quilt*, 1907–1908
Daughters of the Grand Army of the
Republic, Post 28, maker
Cotton
71 × 75 in.
Chicago Historical Society, Decorative and
Industrial Arts Collection, 1987.137

7. Edward T. Hurley
Rookwood Vase, ca. 1909
Glazed stoneware
H. 14 in.
Cooper-Hewitt National Museum of
Design, Smithsonian Institution, New
York, gift of Marsha and William Good-
man, 1984-84-1

8. *Victory—1918*, 1918
United States Tiffany Furnaces, Corona,
Long Island, New York, maker
Transparent iridescent gold and blown,
pressed glass
1⅞ × 7 in.
Corning Museum of Glass, Corning, New
York, 62.4.27

9. Beniamino B. Bufano
Chinese Man and Woman, 1921
Glazed stoneware
31½ × 17½ in.
Metropolitan Museum of Art, New York,
gift of George Blumenthal, 1924

10. *Plaque*, ca. 1924–30
California Faience Company, maker
Glazed earthenware
10½ × 7 in.
Cooper-Hewitt National Museum
of Design, Smithsonian Institution,
New York, gift of Marsha and William
Goodman, 1984-84-53

11. Arthur B. Davies
At the Gates of Morning, ca. 1925
G. La Boure, weaver
G. Montereau atelier, Gobelins factory,
Paris, maker
Wool
69 × 38¼ in.
Memorial Art Gallery, University of
Rochester, New York, gift of Mr. and
Mrs. Niles Meriweather Davies, 62.23

12. René Clarke
Stadium, 1927
Stehli Prints, maker
Printed crepe-de-chine silk
7 × 7 in. (framed swatch)
Newark Museum, New Jersey, Purchase
1927, 27.233

13. John Held, Jr.
Rhapsody, 1927
Stehli Prints, maker
Printed crepe-de-chine silk
7 × 7 in. (framed swatch)
Newark Museum, New Jersey, Purchase
1927, 28.157

14. Victor F. von Lossberg
America, sketch panel for baptismal
font, Christ Church, Cranbrook Acad-
emy, 1927
Edward F. Caldwell and Company, New
York, maker
Enamel on brass
13½ × 9½ in., mounted on velvet-covered
panel measuring 16 × 10½ in.
Cranbrook Academy of Art Museum,
Bloomfield Hills, Michigan, gift of Victor
F. von Lossberg through George C.
Booth, CAAM 1925.36

15. Frederick Carder
*Commemorative Plaque with Intaglio
Portrait of Thomas Alva Edison*, 1929
Steuben Division of Corning Glass
Works, Corning, New York, maker
Cast and pressed glass
8½ × 6½ × ¾ in.
National Museum of American History,
Smithsonian Institution, Washington,
D.C., 69.98

16. Lillian Holm
First Sight of New York, early 1930s
Linen, wool, and cotton
82 × 64⅛ in.
Flint Institute of Arts, Michigan, gift of
the artist in memory of Ralph T. Sayles,
65.14

17. Frank L. Koralewsky
Lock with Hinges and Key, 1932
Carved steel inlaid with brass
13½ × 14¼ in. (lock); h. 9½ in. (hinge)
Cranbrook Academy of Art Museum,
Bloomfield Hills, Michigan, gift of
George and Ellen Booth through the
Cranbrook Foundation, CAAM 1932.3

18. Henry Varnum Poor
Ten Nights in a Bar Room, 1932
Ceramic
16 × 15 in.
Collection of Robert C. Graham, Sr.

19. Eliel and Loja Saarinen
*Sample for the Festival of the May
Queen Hanging*, 1932
Studio Loja Saarinen, maker
Linen warp; linen, wool, and silk weft;
plain weave with discontinuous wefts
86 × 45 in.
Cranbrook Academy of Art Museum,
Bloomfield Hills, Michigan, gift of
Mrs. Adolf Hornblad, CAAM 1979.20

20. Bertha Stenge
Century of Progress Quilt, 1933
Cotton
76 × 76 in.
Chicago Historical Society, Decorative
and Industrial Arts Collection, 1957.33

21. Russell Barnett Aitken
Futility of a Well-ordered Life, 1935
Glazed earthenware
18½ × 7 in. (base)
Museum of Modern Art, New York,
anonymous gift, 1936

22. Domingo Tejada
Chair with Embroidered Cover, 1937
Gold-cream and orange embroidery
and pine
34½ × 15½ × 16½ in.
Collection of Ray and Judy Dewey

23. Edris Eckhardt
Earth, 1939
Glazed earthenware
13 × 8 × 6½ in.
Everson Museum of Art of Syracuse
and Onondaga County, New York, gift of
Dr. Paul Nelson, P.C. 84.30

24. Arthur Nevill Kirk
Triptych with Virgin and Child, ca. 1940
Silver and enamel
9¾ × 4⁷⁄₁₆ in. (closed); 6 in. (open)
Cranbrook Academy of Art Museum,
Bloomfield Hills, Michigan, gift of
George and Ellen Booth through the
Cranbrook Foundation, CAAM 1940.69

25. Viktor Schreckengost
Apocalypse '42, 1942
Glazed ceramic
15³⁄₈ × 20³⁄₈ × 8¹⁄₈ in.
National Museum of American Art,
Smithsonian Institution, Washington,
D.C., gift of the artist, 1985.92.1

26. Sidney Waugh
The Bowl of American Legends, 1942
Steuben Glass Company, maker
Blown and engraved lead crystal
Diam. 10 in.
Collection of Steuben Glass Company,
New York

27. Thomas McClure
Carved Bowl (Passion of Christ), 1947
Stoneware
6³⁄₈ × 6¹⁄₈ in.
Everson Museum of Art of Syracuse and
Onondaga County, New York, Purchase
Prize given by Homer Laughlin China
Company, Thirteenth Ceramic National
Exhibition, 1948, P.C. 49.565

28. Edwin and Mary Scheier
Judgment of Solomon, 1948
Earthenware with matt glazes
Diam. 14½ in.
Newark Museum, New Jersey, Purchase
1949, Special Purchase Fund, 49.370

29. Rudy Autio
Three Musicians, ca. 1952
Clay
20½ × 11 × 9 in.
Collection of Frances Senska

30. Peter Voulkos
Babe, the Blue Ox, ca. 1952
Stoneware
15 × 7 in.
Contemporary Crafts Association,
Portland, Oregon

31. Lenore Tawney
Bound Man, 1957
Wool, silk, linen, and goat hair
84 × 36 in.
American Craft Museum, New York,
Museum Purchase 1957; donated to the
American Craft Museum by the Ameri-
can Craft Council, 1990, 1958.2

32. Joseph Trippetti
Farmer, 1957
Silver and cloisonné enamel on copper
7 × 10 × 2 in.
Minnesota Museum of Art, Saint Paul,
gift of Dayton's, Minneapolis, Minnesota, 57.13.20

33. Tommy Simpson
Flower Garden, 1965
Carved and painted butternut
24 × 44 × 30 in.
Collection of Tommy Simpson

34. J. Fred Woell
The Good Guys, 1966
Walnut, steel, copper, plastic, and silver
Diam. 4 in.
American Craft Museum, New York, gift
of the Johnson Wax Company, from
Objects: USA, 1977; donated to the
American Craft Museum by the Ameri-
can Craft Council, 1990, 77.2.102

35. Howard Kottler
a. *Peace March*, 1967
b. *Sticks, Stones, and Bones*, 1968
Commercial ceramic plates
Diam. 10½ in. (each)
Estate of Howard Kottler

36. Robert Ebendorf
Man and His Pet Bee, 1968
Copper, photo tintype, silver, and
found objects
5 × 3½ in.
Collection of Daphne Farago

37. Michael Frimkess
Jumpin' at the Moon, 1968
Stoneware with overglaze and luster
28¼ × 16 in.
Scripps College, Claremont, California,
gift of Mr. and Mrs. Fred Marer,
SC92.1.3a, b

38. Helena Hernmarck
Talking Trudeau-Nixon, 1969
Wool and nylon
Three panels: 51 × 42–47 in.
Left and right panels: American Craft
Museum, New York, gift of the artist,
1990. Center panel: Collection of Jack
Lenor Larsen, promised gift to the Amer-
ican Craft Museum, New York, 1990.1.2

39. Jack Earl
Untitled, 1969–70
Glazed porcelain
40½ × 34 × 5½ in.
Collection of Thomas L. and Geraldine
Kerrigan

40. Clayton Bailey
Bigfoot Bones, 1971
Stoneware with stain
82 × 24 × 36 in.
Collection of Clayton Bailey

41. Eleanor Moty
Dual Image Pin, 1974
Sterling silver, quartz crystal, and
obsidian star
2 × 2¾ × ¼ in.
Collection of Robert Pfannebecker

42. Patti Warashina
Mother Goosed, 1974
Clay
26 × 16 × 16 in.
Palm Beach Community College, Florida

43. Viola Frey
Junkyard Dreaming, 1975
Whiteware with underglaze and glaze
27 × 28 × 26 in.
Collection of Judith and Martin
Schwartz

44. David Furman
In the Bathroom with Molly, 1975
Earthenware with underglaze, glaze,
luster, and ceramic decals
7 × 8 × 11 in.
Collection of the artist

45. Ed Rossbach
Handgun, 1975
Plaited construction paper
36½ × 50 in.
Craft Alliance, Saint Louis, gift of the
artist, 1992

46. Jim Cotter
Texas Double Dipper, 1976
Cast bronze
7 × 3 in.
Collection of William Crook

47. Martha Glowacki
Overlooking Wells, June, 1977, 1977
Bronze, copper, Plexiglas, paint,
and paper
4 × 3½ × 1¼ in.
Collection of the artist

48. Katherine Westphal
New Treasures of Tutankhamen, 1977–78
Panne velvet, heat-transfer dye, crayons,
and color Xerox
90 × 50 in.
Collection of the artist

49. Richard Notkin
Vain Imaginings, 1978
White earthenware with wood and silver
16 × 13½ × 16½ in.
Los Angeles County Museum of Art,
gift of Howard and Gwen Laurie Smits,
M.87.1.117a–e

50. Martha Banyas
Testimony, 1979
Cloisonné enamel on copper and silver
8½ × 10 × 2 in.
Collection of the artist

51. Audrey Handler
An American Breakfast, 1979
Glass, wood, and silver
7½ × 10⅞ × 14⅞ in.
Collection of Charles Gailis

52. Joan Steiner
Manhattan Collar, 1979
Mixed media
5 × 18 × 7 in.
Courtesy Julie: Artisans' Gallery,
New York

53. Michael Aschenbrenner
22nd Surgical, 1981
Mixed media
40 × 15 × 5 in.
Courtesy Miller Gallery, New York

54. Wendell Castle
Table with Gloves and Keys, 1981
Mahogany
33 × 40 × 16 in.
Forbes Magazine Collection, New York

55. Thomas Lundberg
Dog in the Water, 1981
Cotton and silk embroidery on linen
3½ × 3½ in.
Collection of Darle and Patrick Maveety

56. Esther Luttikhuizen
Sprats, 1981
Mixed media
19½ × 12 × 6 in.
Collection of Dellas Henke

57. Ricky Bernstein
It's Time to Get Up!, 1982
Hand-blown and constructed glass on
aluminum
12 × 12 × 12 in.
Collection of the artist

58. Kenneth Ferguson
Platter with Adam and Eve, 1982
Stoneware with porcelain slip
4½ × 24 in.
Nelson-Atkins Museum of Art,
Kansas City, Missouri, anonymous loan,
34-1982/3

59. Mark Burns
Saint Vitus, 1983
Hand-built earthenware with under-
glaze stains and paint, fluorescent light
41 × 25 × 12 in.
Estate of Howard Kottler

60. D. R. Wagner
The Fingering, 1984
Cotton thread on cotton canvas
5½ × 15¼ in.
Collection of Bruce and Jacqueline
Whitelam

61. Joyce J. Scott
*Eaten Alive: South Africa's Greatest
Fear,* 1986
Beads on wire support
9½ × 2½ × 6¼ in.
Collection of Dorothy May Campbell

62. Dana Boussard
*We Met with Oh, Such Separate
Dreams,* 1987
Cut, painted, and sewn fiber construc-
tion; canvas backed flat cotton and vel-
vet
53 × 116 in.
Collection of the artist

63. Jan Holcomb
Two Worlds, 1987
Stoneware with oil paint
35 × 28 in.
Collection of Mr. and Mrs. Randolph
A. Marks

64. Gerhardt Knodel
Guardians of the New Day, 1987
Painted and printed cotton tapes, woven
with mixed-media elements
93 × 186 × 6 in. (overall)
Collection of the artist

65. Arturo Alonzo Sandoval
*State of the Union No. 10—Lady Lib-
erty's Centennial Celebration,* 1987
Silk, color Xerox transfers, metallic and
monofilament threads, and rayon
63 × 90 in.
Collection of Mr. and Mrs. R. J. Vaccarella

66. Kiff Slemmons
a. *Roald Amundsen,* 1987
Sterling silver and acrylic
Collection of Garth Clark and Mark
Del Vecchio
b. *Jacques Cousteau,* 1988
Sterling silver, acrylic, and shell
Collection of Gretchen Adkins
c. *Emily Dickinson,* 1988
Sterling silver, brass, and watch face
Collection of Virginia Wright
d. *Houdini,* 1987
Sterling silver
Collection of Mrs. Virginia Holshuh
e. *Don Quixote,* 1989
Sterling silver and leather
Collection of Mrs. Virginia Holshuh
H. 3¼ in. (each)

67. Judy Jensen
Denial, 1988
Reverse painting on glass with
mixed media
39 × 34 in.
Collection of the artist

68. Paul Marioni
Hiroshima, 1988
Cast glass
11⁵⁄₁₆ × 9 × 2 in.
Courtesy William Traver Gallery, Seattle

69. Robert Arneson
a. *Chief Executive Officer,* 1989
b. *Rapist and Drug Dealer,* 1989
Glazed ceramic
25 × 12 × 12 in. (each)
Courtesy Frumkin/Adams Gallery,
New York, FA82-5019, FA82-5018

70. Bruce Metcalf
A Present from the Government, 1989
Silver, Plexiglas, and Mylar
3¼ × 3½ × ¾ in.
Courtesy Susan Cummins Gallery,
Mill Valley, California

71. Ronna Neuenschwander
N'na and Her Can, 1990
Adobe, earthenware, metal, and wood
60 × 44 × 14 in.
Courtesy Susan Cummins Gallery,
Mill Valley, California

72. Terrie Hancock Mangat
Desert Storm, 1991
100 percent cotton-rag paper, electric
blanket, hand-pieced and hand-quilted
cotton and silk fabrics
96 × 84 in.
Collection of the artist

73. Alan Stirt
War Bowl, 1991
Ceanothus burl, turned and scorched
5¾ × 9 in.
Wood Turning Center, Philadelphia

ACKNOWLEDGMENTS

An exhibition of this magnitude, along with its accompanying catalogue, its national tour, and its related community education programs, is inevitably a collaborative effort on the part of many people and institutions. We are indebted to the lenders and artists who made the work in Tales & Traditions available. We want to pay particular thanks to the volunteer Steering Committee who guided us through the labyrinthine process of organizing, funding, and promoting this effort: Dr. Leigh Gerdine, who chaired the committee, Marylen Mann, Donna Nussbaum, Frank Roth, Sissy Thomas, Jo Jasper, Peter Mackie, Phyllis Langsdorf, JoAnne Kohn, Ruth Siteman, Richard Gaddes, David Mesker, Ronnie Greenberg, Barbara Wagman, Judith Aronson, Sarah Russell, Noel Leicht, and Jay Lawrence, and Julie McClennan. To the entire Board of Directors, staff, and faculty of Craft Alliance we extend our sincere appreciation for your encouragement, support, guidance, and hard work to ensure the success of Tales and Traditions. In particular, we are indebted to Barbara Jedda, Chief Curator of Craft Alliance from 1990-1993 for three years of unstinting effort and devoted work on the exhibition; to Harriet Traurig for her curatorial expertise; to Lorilee Richardson, former Education Director of Craft Alliance for conceptualizing educational programming around the exhibition, and to Barbara-Decker Franklin, Craft Alliance Program Director for successfully designing and implementing those ambitious educational goals; and to Jean Marie Deken for her careful proofreading of the catalogue text. We also acknowledge the many contributions made by the Washington University Gallery of Art, its Director, Joe Ketner, and its registrar, Marie Nordman.

This exhibition, its related public programs, and national tour is organized by Craft Alliance and made possible by a major grant from the Lila Wallace-Reader's Digest Fund.

Additional support for this exhibition and related Year of American Craft programming has been provided by the Goldstein National Endowment for the Arts, a federal agency; The Missouri Arts Council, a state agency; the St. Louis Regional Arts Commission; the Goldsmith Foundation, the Arts and Education Council of Greater St. Louis; Elleard B. Heffern, Inc.; Venture Stores, Inc.; The May Department Stores Company and its Famous-Barr Division; The Trio Foundation; Mark Twain Bancshares, Inc.; The William T. Kemper Foundation; the Moog Charitable Trust; Monsanto Company; Anheuser-Busch; Silver Dollar City, Inc.; Ronald McDonald Childrens Charities; Blueberry Hill; Meli-Melo; and Vintage Vinyl; an anonymous donor; and many individual contributors. Special acknowledgements are due to Marquand Books, Inc. for their role in designing the exhibition catalogue; to the University of Washington Press, for catalogue distribution; to Frank Roth Direct Marketing for catalogue publication; to John Stark Printing Company, Inc. for catalogue printing; to Purk Prepress, Inc. for color separations and film preparation and to Smith-Kramer Fine Art Services for the handling of the national tour of the exhibition.

Individual patrons and contributors to the exhibition included: Donna & William Nussbaum, Mr. & Mrs. Keith Shaw, Pete Fischer ,Bill & Ellen Livingston, Mr. & Mrs. Julian Seeherman, John Weil, Mr. & Mrs. Mont Levy, Earl Shreckengast & Julia Muller,Mr. & Mrs.David Wahl, Bob Fox & Maxine Clark, Mr. & Mrs. Herbert Smith, Peter Bunce, Mr. & Mrs. John Isaacs, Mr. & Mrs. Richard Baizer, Mike Scully, Bill & Jeanne Casey, Helen Weiss, Mr. & Mrs. Stuart Zimmerman , Mr. & Mrs. Walter Schmitz, Mr. & Mrs. Jerry Baer, Mr. & Mrs. Bruce White, Mr. & Mrs. Kenneth Langsdorf, Pat Heller, Sarah Russell, Dr. & Mrs. Bruce McClennan, Mr. & Mrs. Richard Marx, Patti & J.B. Cohn, Alan & Joanne Kohn , Richard Gaddes, David Mesker, Paul Forman, and Mrs. Louis Chubb.

James R. Reed
Executive Director